A MAN

CALLED

GEORGE

GOD CAN MAKE YOU STRONG

IN YOUR SPIRITUAL WALK

GEORGE M. DUGGAN, JR.

Unless otherwise indicated, all scripture quotations are taken from the New American Bible translated from the original languages with critical use of all the ancient sources by members of the Catholic Bible Association of America, sponsored by the Bishop's Committee of the Confraternity of Christian Doctrine.

A MAN CALLED GEORGE

Copyright © 2004

ISBN Number: 0-939241-56-0

George M. Duggan, Jr.
46 Queen Street #12
Charleston, SC 29401

Printed in the United States of America.

DEDICATION

I dedicate this book to my wife, Sara, who has been by my side for all these decades...the adventure continues.

I dedicate this book to the faith of St. Patrick that is not only my personal heritage, but the power that he sought and received has inspired many faithful throughout centuries.

I dedicate this book to all my Christian friends who are still seeking their personal Savior.

I dedicate this book to all of my friends who have prayed for me over the years. How can I say "thank you" enough for your perseverance.

I dedicate this book to committed Full Gospel businessmen who continue to put the Lord first in their business.

I acknowledge the assistance in this book of my friend, Bob Armstrong.

A MAN CALLED GEORGE

TABLE OF CONTENTS

A MAN CALLED GEORGE

FOREWORD

DR. FRED LADENIUS

A Man Called George is the engaging and inspiring autobiography of an unusual man. George Duggan outlines in a clear and simple language the impact that an encounter with the extraordinary life giving power of the Holy Spirit can have on any person regardless of their background or religious affiliation. In the early 1970's, after receiving the Baptism of the Holy Spirit and having become involved in the Catholic Charismatic Renewal, I had just got used to the label interdenominational. I remember being struck by a far more significant term: *transdenominational,* a word which Demos Shakarian used during our first meeting in Rome, when I had a chance of speaking with him during a Full Gospel Business Men's Fellowship International airlift. It was some time later at a FGBMFI World Convention that I first met George Duggan.

The following summer I experienced first hand this charismatic, transdenominational power which George's book exhudes page after page, when I attended my first FGBMFI world convention in Anaheim in 1974.

It should be a cause for reflection for us Europeans to think that the Fellowship was born in the United States through Demos Shakarian, who by his blood ties and traditions still lived with one foot in his ancestral Armenia. I became very much aware of these ties when I accompanied him as a translator to the Armenian Church in Paris.

The Renewal which had started in the USA was received by the old and static European Catholic Church, after having been foretold by a prophet called Pope John XXIII. George's book is a valuable and fascinating chronicle of these past thirty years.

Fred Ladenius

A MAN CALLED GEORGE

PREFACE

DR. RICHARD SHAKARIAN

George and Sara Duggan have been our personal friends for over 25 years. As an International Director, George has been greatly instrumental in building the Full Gospel Business Men's Fellowship International to become the world's largest Christian Business fellowship.

A humble and true servant of God is how I would characterize the man called George.

George was trained as an attorney, successful in real estate, and outstanding in investments. However, his legacy goes far beyond the professional world.

The vision that George and Sara have followed is as spiritually exhilarating as the work of Michael Angelo on the ceiling of the Sistine Chapel depicting the hand of God touching the hand of Adam.

He has always been very perceptive, but the Holy Spirit gave him great compassion and focused his attention on helping others. George joined our Fire Team to Nicaragua, at that time, he was 75 years of age. His vision had not grown dim and his energy was very strong. After that week, George said, "I have introduced more people to Christ this week, than in the past 25 years."

His greatest joy is to help others receive the same

fullness of life through our precious Lord.

George and Sara are a real inspiration to Vangie and I.

--Richard Shakarian, International President
  Full Gospel Business Men's Fellowship International

A MAN CALLED GEORGE

Introduction

St. Patrick's Cross

During the third week in May 2001, sixty Americans, people from seven other countries, and hundreds of British had one of the greatest outreaches that the Full Gospel Business Men's Fellowship International (FGBMFI) in England has ever undertaken. It was very successful. While that was going on a small group of us from America were speaking at meetings in Ireland that FGBMFI members had set up for us. These were planning meetings, telling them about Fire Team meetings and how they could have this type of outreach in the future. While there I spoke at the Tralee, County Kerry Chapter, the place my grandparents came from in 1858.

My wife Sara and I visited St. Patrick's Rock of Cashel. The traditional story has it that St. Patrick was ministering here in the year 448 AD. St. Patrick lived from about 389 to 461. The Rock of Cashel rising so commandingly over the central plain must have offered a splendid site for a fortress from the earliest times. The buildings which crown St. Patrick's Rock present a mass and outline of great interest and beauty hardly equaled in these islands. The complex has a character of its own, unique and native, and is one of the most remarkable in Europe.

Cashel first came into prominence in the fourth or fifth century A.D. as the royal seat of the Edghanacht, who claimed lordship over the southern half of Ireland. The main importance of Cashel, however, in the early historic period was as the royal seat of Munster.

It was either Oenghus, son of Nad Fraioch, or his brother and predecessor Corc who was king when St. Patrick ministered at Cashel in about 448. Oenghus's name is traditionally associated with St. Patrick, who is said to have inadvertently pierced the king's foot with his pastoral staff while he was baptizing him. The king, believing this to be an essential part of the ceremony, suffered it without flinching. At the age of 16, Patrick was in slavery in Ireland tending the flocks of a chieftain in Ulster. After six years, he escaped to France and became a monk.

In 432, a vision led Patrick to return to Ireland as a missionary bishop. He worked zealously in various parts of the island for the rest of his life. His labors were so successful that he came to be known as one who "found Ireland all heathen and left it all Christian." He founded over 300 churches and baptized more than 120,000 persons. Many legends grew up about this popular saint.

He left a sort of autobiography in his testimony (or confession) written in Latin. Much study has been given to Saint Patrick, but little that goes beyond the testimony of his own writings can be accepted as certain.

He was buried at Down Cathedral in the city of Downpatrick. In the graveyard there is a huge rock slab bearing the name of the saint, spelled Patric.

After the death of Patrick, the growth of Christianity in Ireland and surrounding areas did not slow down. With over 300 churches, established by Patrick, and the many monasteries, monks and other works of the Spirit, Christianity was moving in Ireland.

The works of Saint Patrick, Columba, Brendan, Adaman and many others did not come by happenstance. They were filled with the Holy Spirit. This was the same power that came on the 120 in the upper room on the day of Pentecost. How else could it happen? The Holy Spirit power was still flourishing in the days of these saints. The gifts of the Holy Spirit are very helpful in evangelism.

After St. Patrick, Columba was a very prominent figure in building Christianity. Columba was born at Gratan in Ireland on December 7, 521 AD. He went to the monastic school of the Abbot Finnian, one of the most famous in Ireland, founded in 520 AD. He was ordained as a priest at Colard, by Bishop Etchen. Columba founded the monastery of Derry, his first one, in the year 545. Between 545 AD and 562 AD, he founded many churches and monasteries. St. Columba lived from 521 to 597.

His accounts and testimonies were written by Saint Adaman, around 679 to 704, as told to him by eyewitnesses. These accounts were translated from the Latin by Bishop Mac Carthy of Kerry, and several others. There are many eyewitness accounts of his amazing prophetic gift. There were many miracles, which included raising the dead and angelic visitations.

Columba established the monastery of Kells in Meath. In this monastery a very famous book was written. It is known as the *Book of Kells*. The ornamentation of the writing is very original, particularly its pictures and scrolling. It is still in existence and is kept in a glass vault at Trinity College in Dublin. Sara and I visited there to see the book.

Columba was very instrumental in moving Christianity to Scotland, by establishing a monastery and a church there on the Isle of Iona.

The gospel of Mark 16:17 says, *"These signs will accompany those who believe: in my name they will drive out demons, they will speak with new languages, they will pick up serpents, and if they drink any deadly thing, it will not harm them. They will lay hands on the sick, and they will recover."*

The reason we do not see these signs attending or following us in the church today is because most of us do not have this Holy Spirit power which we receive through the Baptism in the Holy Spirit. We need it for the gifts of the Spirit to work in our daily lives.

The working of the gifts of the Spirit attracts the un-churched and un-saved persons, so then when we get their attention we can do what Jesus said in Luke 24:47, *"AND THAT REPENTANCE, for the forgiveness of sins, would be preached in his name to all the nations, beginning from Jerusalem."*

This is how Jesus attracted the crowds. Peter also attracted a crowd and preached with very many other words. He said, *"Repent and be baptized, every one of you, in the name of Jesus Christ for the forgiveness of your sins; and you will receive the gift of the holy Spirit. Those who accepted his message were baptized, and about three thousand persons were added that day." Acts 2:38 & 41.*

Everyone, whether it be St. Patrick, Columba, kings,

presidents, businessmen, workers, you and me---needs to receive the promise of the Father and the power of his message in Acts 1:4,5, & 8. Here Jesus commands 120, and us today, not to leave Jerusalem, or wherever we are to go to minister, or preach, until we receive the promise of the Father.

God—always has a plan.

Man—always thinks he has a better idea!

"Obedience is better than sacrifice . . . for a sin like divination is rebellion, and presumption is the crime of idolatry . . ." I Samuel 15:22-23. The promise of the Father is the power we all need to be witnesses for him everywhere they go including the uttermost parts of the earth.

Jesus says that no man can do this ministry in his own power. We must have the Holy Spirit power to get the job done. Being obedient to the Father is the greatest thing we can do because he will show us how to do it, and we will get it accomplished. Even Jesus needed the power of the Holy Spirit for his ministry on earth. If he needed this power, where does it leave us if we do not have it?

When Bishop Nicholas D'Antonio (see chapter 9) received the Baptism of the Holy Spirit, he stirred up a hornet's nest. His ministry was much more successful. The governing authorities even tried to kill him. They did not succeed because he was protected by the hand of the Lord.

Through salvation, we receive a *measure* of the Holy Spirit, but with the Baptism of the Holy Spirit we are *filled* with the Holy Spirit.

The purpose of this book is to share my testimony of how I met the Lord Jesus Christ and how I came to know Him. Also, how I came to be immersed into the promise of the Father, "...*this is what was spoken through the prophet Joel: It will come to pass in the last days, God says, that I will pour out a portion of my spirit upon all flesh.*" Acts 2:16-17.

When I started thinking about what part to put in writing, I started to see that so many highly unusual things had happened to me.

But I did have a strong leading of the Holy Spirit to write my testimony. I had gone to church all my life and then when I was 27 years old I had a salvation experience.

I was just finishing up with law school. What a change that was. Not only did I receive salvation, but I was instantly healed of a painful back injury, and in a few years received four additional major miracle healings. At this point in time I had a strong desire to read and study the Bible, which I never even thought about before.

The very centerpiece of the book will come from the five times the Holy Spirit spoke to me in an audible voice. This happened in 1968, when I was forty-one years old, living in Baltimore, Maryland at 1216 Sherwood Avenue with my wife Sara and four sons. Our youngest son was one year old that year.

At four o'clock in the morning, I woke up and sat up in bed, hearing a loud, audible voice speaking to me. One of the statements was that Richard Nixon would be the next president of the United States.

A few months later, the Holy Spirit spoke to me; he said that there were many people in my church denomination who were church members only. They did not have salvation. I had just studied the Bible for approximately eight years, and I was trying to understand that statement.

The Holy Spirit showed me that I had a sister and a brother who were not saved. At my mother's funeral I was instrumental in leading my sister into salvation. My brother later received salvation also.

At the time I was running two businesses, one in Baltimore and one in Charleston, traveling there monthly and spending two days there each time. The Holy Spirit showed me that the problem of many in the church not being saved was the cause and root problem of other problems that you could see. But this was the largest and main problem that the church had. It even contributed greatly to the recent sex scandal in the church.

Starting in the early 1990's, the Holy Spirit and the Bishop of Rome have been tugging on the church to move into a meaningful evangelistic program. The book will address that problem and how to correct the situation of many that are unsaved in the Church.

The Baptism of the Holy Spirit, which is needed for all ministry in the church, is told about in Acts 2:15-17, described in Acts 2:4, and set out in Matthew 3:11, Mark 1:8, Luke 3:16, John 1:33, and Acts 1:5. The gifts of the Holy Spirit are stated in I Corinthians 12:8-9. They only work through receiving the Baptism of the Holy Spirit. Acts 10:38 tells us *"how God anointed Jesus of Nazareth with the Holy Spirit and power."* If Jesus needed this Holy

Spirit power for his ministry here on earth, how much more do we need this power for the five-fold ministry, which includes evangelism and the work of the church today.

In Acts 1:4 and 8, while meeting with the apostles, Jesus enjoined them not to depart from Jerusalem and go out to minister until they had received the Baptism of the Holy Spirit and power, and this carries over to our ministering today. Our leadership, bishops, pastors, preachers, priests, evangelists, missionaries, and all other lay persons who have ministries in the Church, must have this power for the church to be spiritually successful today. That is what Jesus is telling us. Obedience to our heavenly Father, the Son Jesus, and the Holy Spirit is the greatest thing that we can do, and by doing this we will receive the greatest blessing in the church and in our ministry.

The Baptism in the Holy Spirit has always been available to the church. Yet for the past several hundred years I have not been able to find where anyone in our church denomination had this blessing. That is up until August of 1960, when Pope John 23rd sent his representative to the meeting of the commission on faith and order of the World Council of Churches in St. Andrews, Scotland. His representative brought back a good report. In March of 1967 nine Notre Dame University students went to a prayer meeting at Ray Bullard's home. He was a Director of the Full Gospel Business Men's Fellowship International. There they received the Baptism of the Holy Spirit. Not only did this happen at Notre Dame, but about the same time this Pentecostal experience was being poured out for the first time on young lay persons at Duquesne and several other colleges. There they received the Baptism of the Holy Spirit. In 1975, a group of 10,000 people with this blessing met at the Vatican.

I was in a meeting at the Vatican on March 25, 2003 and was told by Director Oreste Pesare of International Renewal services that there are now 120,000,000 in the church worldwide today with this blessing.

I can clearly see that the major problem that we have in this church denomination is that there are many of our members who do not have salvation, just as the Holy Spirit said. I believe that I can clearly show this from the Scripture in the Bible for all to see.

I would hope that this book would be a help to many of the people in our church. I would like to see many of those who the Holy Spirit said did not have salvation to have that closer walk with the Lord and Savior Jesus Christ. It was difficult for me to understand at first when the Holy Spirit said that. I had always thought in the past, that when you become a church member, that you have salvation.

I have been doing evangelistic work now for over 28 years. I have seen many come to the Lord in Nicaragua, Honduras and El Salvador. I have worked in a number of other countries, including the United States, as a layman doing evangelistic work. It is my hope that I could be of some help to the Church. To my heavenly Father, I give all the glory!

A MAN CALLED GEORGE

Early Overcomings

My grandparents, John James Duggan and Mary Agnes O'Connell, came from Tralee, County Kerry, Ireland a short while before they were married at St. Patrick's Roman Catholic Church, on November 14, 1858, in Charleston, South Carolina. My father said that his mother was a grand niece of Daniel O'Connell, the Irish lawyer and statesman, member of the British Parliament and a mayor of Dublin.

My father, George Michael Duggan Sr., was the youngest of eight children born to his parents on October 3, 1876. Dad's home was at 46 Queen Street, Charleston, South Carolina, where he lived with two of his sisters. He was a fireman in the late 19th century and early 20th century and a Charleston policeman from the years of 1908 to 1924. In 1924 when John P. Grace lost the election for mayor to Tom Stoney, dad resigned from the police force and went to Florida to see an orange grove that his sister Annie had just bought.

While in St. Joseph, Florida, he met my mother on a neighboring orange grove. They were married in St. Joseph's Catholic Church in 1926, and they made their home there. My Dad was a few months short of his fiftieth birthday and mother was thirty-two when they married.

I was born in 1927, the oldest of six children. My father died on March 5, 1942, when I was fifteen years old and in the third year of high school. In June, at the end of my third year of high school, I asked my mother if I could go to work for a few years to support the family. Later I would go back and finish school. Mother allowed me to do this.

SHIPBUILDING

I went to Charleston, South Carolina where I took a course in shipbuilding at the National Youth Administration School in North Charleston for defense workers.

I found a job at the Southeastern Shipbuilding Corp. in Savannah, Georgia and went to work on October 17, 1942. For the rest of 1942, 1943, and 1944, I worked as a shipfitter, building ships for the war effort.

I felt I was a part of the war effort in those days. My father had just died, and I needed to make a living. I was the oldest of a family of six children. My youngest brother was only about three or four. My mother could not get out and work. She still had an orange grove, but it had been tied up in a lawsuit for five years. There was not any income coming, because they leased it again to pay off the attorneys, despite winning the case. Even though I was only 15 years old, I felt like I needed to go to work to support the family, which I did.

It paid good money. My last job in Florida before shipbuilding was only paying $7 a week, one dollar a day.

My first week in the shipyard, I made $100. I jumped from $7 a week to $100 a week. I could support my family that way.

I was even able to save some money so I could go back to school and go to college after World War Two.

MY WORK ETHIC

The work ethic that I have probably came from my family, more from my mother than my father. On my mother's side of the family, she was German; my father's side was Irish. Up until the time I was 15 years old, we just didn't sit around on Saturdays or holidays; we had to get out of the house and do a job. If we didn't have a job to do, my mother would find a job for us.

I must confess that a lot of the times I did not like the jobs that she would find for me, so I would go ahead and find something that I would like to do better. As long as I was busy, she didn't have anything to say. I was also staying out of trouble.

My "work ethic" was instilled within us as young people. That is one of the things I believe. To be successful in business, today, you need a work ethic. You need to find a work that you like to do; then you will be happy in that work, you become more prosperous in that type of work, because you are doing what you like to do. It is important with both men and women to find a kind of work that you like to do, early in life. Then you will have a much happier and more successful life, because your work is almost like a hobby.

A good work ethic is very important. First, you need

to find something that you like to do. Then you need to educate yourself about it. You need to go further in school or college to learn about it. Take special education in that field. Then, concentrate on it. Try to be the best that you can be in that particular business. If it's a service, if you are benefiting people, then you will be profitable in your business, you'll have satisfaction in your business because you like what you are doing, and you will become successful in that particular field.

You want to be the best that you can in whatever you do, especially as a Christian. And you will have tremendous success in life. You will have spiritual and physical success in the world, as people see you. You will be a good witness for the Lord Jesus Christ.

In 1945 the day before I was eighteen years old, I enlisted in the United States Navy and I served about fifteen months until I was discharged shortly after the end of World War II. I went back to high school for the 1946-47 school year and graduated.

In 1947 I went to Baltimore, Maryland where I could work and go to college also. I worked in three different shipyards, The Maryland Drydock Co., Key Highway Lower Shipyard, and Key Highway (Bethlehem Steel) Ship Repair Yard, as a shipfitter, which was my trade.

While working in the shipyard, I attended college and law school. I graduated from law school in 1954 and obtained a Juris Doctorate degree from the University of Baltimore.

When I was in the last year of law school, I left the

shipyard and went to work for the William C. Rogers Law Firm and his Title Guarantee Co., known as The Security Title Guarantee Corp., for two years. The last year I taught new lawyers how to search real estate titles.

INTEREST IN REAL ESTATE

I left the legal field for four years in 1956 and started a real estate investment business back in Charleston. Then for ten years, 1960 through 1970, I worked in the legal field, the real estate title business, in Baltimore. In 1970, I went full-time into the real estate investment business.

When I first started in the real estate investment business, I restored a very old building that was about 150 years old at that time. I liked to do that. It became a very lucrative business in real estate.

I cannot remember where I got the first idea to go into the real estate business. When I went to Baltimore and went to law school, I studied law to learn how to buy real estate with no money down. But I did want to know, to have a legal background, so I could handle the business of it. My family owned orange groves down in Florida, and they had problems with both of them, legal problems, which cost them a lot of money. I figured out that if I knew what the law was, I would be much more successful. I studied business administration and law. It would help me in the business of real estate, which I had intended to get into right away.

Then I got side-tracked. Actually, after law school, I came to Charleston to buy my property. I set up my first 11 apartments. When I was paying off the first mortgage here (I had gotten married in the meantime and had one child), we went back to Baltimore and I worked in the legal field where I started a title company for lawyers. I worked in that for about eight of the ten years in Baltimore the second time. We had to do all that traveling, ten trips a year.

I asked the Lord, "Which business should I stay in?" The Lord spoke to me in 1968, "I want you to pick up your family and move back to Charleston." I said, "Okay, Lord, but I will need some extra money to make this move with loss of some of my income." Shortly after that, an elderly lady died. I settled her estate, but I bought the property with no money down, and it could be held in the estate until I found a buyer for it. So I improved it and sold it. I put $17,500 in my pocket out of that deal.

Using my work ethic and perseverance, and with God's mercy and help, I overcame many obstacles during the early roads of life.

A MAN CALLED GEORGE

From a Life Without Purpose
To a Life of TRANSFORMATION

In 1954 when I was in law school, I rented a room in Baltimore from Howard and Grace Chatham. Howard Chatham was in the army in France in World War I. His outfit was wiped out two and one-half times. All the men were replaced except Chatham, who was the only original man left from the original group. In World War II, he was a chief engineer on merchant ships. He got off of three different ships after the last trip each one made before they were sunk. Some may have called him "lucky," but I later found out that God had spared his life for a purpose.

When I first met Mr. Chatham, he was very sick with a bad heart condition, so bad that he could not work. I understood that the doctor had only given him a short time to live. A couple from a Pentecostal church prayed for his healing, and after that he was back working around the house again.

Grace was a Southern Baptist, but Chatham did not belong to any church. After he was healed, he started spending a lot of time reading the Bible. That year after the healing incident, Oral Roberts came to Baltimore with his large tent and healing crusade.

Howard and Grace went to the Oral Roberts' meetings every night for the nine nights that his team were in Baltimore. Since Howard was healed he had become very interested in faith healing. In the evenings, he would tell me about the healing meetings and the many physical healings that he could see. He spoke of lame people walking again; blind people seeing again; deaf people hearing again; and many other healings that he saw take place.

Several months later another healing evangelist, by the name of Tommy Hicks, came to Baltimore. Howard asked me if I would like to go to a meeting and see some healing miracles. I told him I certainly would like to do that.

When I was about seven years old, another young person hit me across the back with a large stick and injured some vertebraes in my back. We were playing in a pile of leaves and when I was hit I could not get up right away. It was several months before I could run again without it hurting. As a teenager, I had many backaches. Now I was twenty-seven and from time to time I had serious pain in my back.

The night we went to the meeting, I had worked in the shipyard all day and my back was tired and hurting. As we walked about six blocks to the meeting, each time we crossed a street, I stepped down from the curb easy to keep my back from hurting even more.

Before Tommy Hicks preached he talked about a tremendous healing crusade that he had just come from in Argentina. Now there were many Catholics living in Argentina and Juan D. Peron was the president of the country at that time. Tommy said that the Lord spoke to him and told him to go to Argentina and hold this crusade. The first thing he did in Argentina was to go to the presidential Palace to see Peron. Peron would not see him though.

When the doorman came to the door and told him that Peron would not see him, the doorman was limping, and his ankle was tied up in a bandage. Tommy asked him what was the matter with his foot. He said it had been injured and would not heal because he was a diabetic. He asked the doorman if he could pray for his foot. The doorman said yes, and as Tommy prayed for his foot, it was totally healed that instant. Then he said go tell Peron what happened and ask him if I could see him now. The doorman came back in a little while and said Peron will see you, and an appointment was set up for the meeting.

When Tommy went in to see Peron he found out that Peron was having a problem with very unsightly splotches on his face. The doctor thought it was the first stages of leprosy. Peron asked Tommy if he could pray for his face. Tommy said he would pray for him and when he prayed for Peron's face it changed right before their eyes. The skin on his face became as smooth as a baby's skin— and beautifully healed. After that he asked Tommy what he wanted.

He asked him for the use of some of the largest stadiums around the country to hold crusades, and for the use of some radio stations to announce the meetings. His desire was that many of his people be healed, but also that many thousands of his Catholic people would make a deeper commitment of their lives to the Lord. This would be a great help for his country. This request was granted, and for several months thousands filled those large stadiums in Argentina.

This was part of the great healing revivals that started right after World War II and moved around the world. I later went to a William Branham meeting in Washington, D.C., a short while after the Tommy Hicks Baltimore meeting. William Branham was known for praying for persons with cancer who became healed. Some of the ones who were well known at this period of time were Oral Roberts, Tommy Hicks, William Branham, and A. A. Allan, but there were many others also.

I was told by Bob French, a South African businessman who moved to the United States, that when William Branham came to Durban, South Africa, for a healing crusade that he visited the hospitals, and that every sick person in every hospital in the city of Durban was healed, and the hospitals where empty. He said it was in all of the newspapers and that the doctors were upset by it. As I have since traveled in numerous countries, I know that the world is full of desperate people; and desperate people MUST SEE the miracle-working power of God.

Tommy Hicks preached on Ezekiel Chapter 37. After he preached he told the people that whoever needed healing for anything should get in a line. He was going to pray for them and God was going to heal them.

I was not familiar with this kind of meeting, but as soon as he said those words about healing, and without thinking about it, I found myself in that healing line. And when I got about ten feet from where he was praying, it felt like electricity was in the air. It passed through my body and the pain left. I was totally healed at that moment, and my back is still healed to this day. I stayed in the line and Tommy Hicks prayed for me.

But that was not all that happened to me, for the next morning I found that I was changed. I was different than I had ever been before. I had not thought about reading a Bible before, but that next morning I wanted a Bible and I wanted to read it more than anything else. This was an experience from the Lord that no one can take away from me.

More than anything else I believe it to be a salvation experience. I always had attended church regularly, but it was more from a sense of duty. Now I wanted to know the Lord.

Before I was saved, I did go by what I was told. It was the right thing to do---to go to church. One needed to go to church on Sunday to be able to live a good life, and to go to heaven when one died. There wasn't much else that I understood about salvation. Good advice is what I heard from parents and teachers, people who I thought were good people.

Of course life was a total change after that night, the night of my salvation. It is difficult to put into words, but I knew that there was a great change. First of all, on that particular evening when I received Jesus as Lord and Savior of my life, I was healed.

I had a lot of pain and backaches as a teenager and in my early twenties. That was instantly healed and gone. I felt the power of God when that miracle happened. There was a surge of electricity in the air. This power went through my body and the pain left. I felt the power of God, which the Bible calls the anointing of God. I wanted all that God had for me, including to immerse myself into the holy scriptures, God's Word.

Some time passed before I received the Bible I wanted, but when I did, I spent much time reading and studying God's Word.

I always believed in miracles. I always believed that God would heal you. But I thought there would be special people with special gifts who had to pray for you. I didn't realize that I could learn how to pray for myself for healing. That was a big surprise that I would be doing it.

Even though I had the desire to pray for others and have them healed, I was learning that from the scriptures. The more that I would read from the scriptures, the stronger I would get in my belief. This blessing kept getting better and better all of the time.

The biggest way I changed after salvation was because of reading the Bible. I understood much, much clearer about the Word of God, about the Bible, about salvation, about being born again, and all those spiritual things that Jesus talked about in the Bible, and in that particular part, salvation is given to us in detail in the New Testament. I felt that I just came into the understanding of how salvation worked. It just became more clear to me each day, and each time that I read the scriptures.

I still look back at the experience that I had at the healing evangelistic meeting with Tommy Hicks in 1954. As I went forward that night in faith believing that Jesus would heal me, something else happened that was even more life-changing than the healing of my back.

I asked Jesus to come into my heart and take over my life, and He did that night. Because of that I had a salvation experience, which became a personal relationship with the King of Kings and Lord of Lords.

We must ask Him to come into our hearts. We must confirm, ourselves, what happened earlier in our lives before we reached the age of reason, after we become adults.

If we don't ask Him to come into our hearts, He won't do it. He will not push his way in like the enemy. We must ask Him; we must invite Him into our hearts. Then and only then will he come into our hearts, and then He will change us. We will have a personal relationship with Him, and we will start to grow spiritually—and become more like Him. Salvation must come first; then we will start to grow spiritually.

We can study about Him all of our lives and know about him. We will fool a lot of people, including ourselves, but we will not have a personal relationship with Him. We will not know Him until we have salvation. When we have salvation His Word, the Holy Bible, will be different to us. The scriptures will be more meaningful and real than before salvation.

After salvation, if you seek God and look for Him diligently through His Word, He will speak to you and talk to you, and there will be a relationship like father and son. He really knows us and cares for us. His Word tells us that He knows the number of hairs on our heads. The Holy Spirit started teaching me about salvation after He spoke to me about it.

My life was totally changed. As I observed my brothers, they just watched to see what was happening in my life. They watched me very closely. They probably thought it would last just a short while, or that salvation and healing were just a "passing fancy." I'm sure they thought to themselves, "Oh, he will get over it." But as I persisted, and I always saw my family at least once a year, I would usually witness to them until the time that they had gotten saved and they had a closer walk with the Lord.

They saw that things were happening in my life that they had not seen before. We had a very close-knit family. We were always in church on Sunday. I was doing real well in business. My business was prospering. After he saw how I was doing in the real estate investment business, one of my brothers actually went into the same business in Florida. We've always been a very close family.

My brothers now spent a lot of time reading their Bibles. They watched a lot of television evangelists. They started growing spiritually. Like me, they grew in their church, because it was "the thing to do."

My life had gone from a life without purpose, to a literally transformed life.

In John 1:1 it says, "In the beginning was the word, and the word was with God, and the Word was God." He was in the beginning with God. All things came to be through him, and without him nothing came to be.

This is telling me that God and his Word are one. The Bible is truly the inspired Word of God, from Genesis to Revelation, that the Word is one of Jesus' names. Then the 14th verse says, "And the Word became flesh and made his dwelling among us, and we saw his glory, the glory as of the Father's only Son, full of grace and truth." And this is telling me that Jesus was there with the Father in Genesis 1:1 which says, "In the beginning, when God created the heavens and the earth…"

I can't begin to put the glory of God into words. After I received salvation at the age of twenty-seven, all these things and more exploded into my mind when I read John's gospel. Nicodemus asked Jesus a question in John 3:4. "How can a person once grown old be born again?" In verse 5 and 6 Jesus answered, "Amen, Amen, I say to you, no one can enter the kingdom of God without being born of water and the Spirit. What is born of flesh is flesh, and what is born of the Spirit is Spirit." What is the water of the new birth? What does the water of the new birth mean? Does it refer to being baptized in water? That is not what Jesus is talking about. The Word of God is the water referred to in John 3:5. We can prove this by going through and reading a number of Scriptures.

A MAN CALLED GEORGE

3

A Woman Called Sara

In 1956 after law school, I went back to Charleston for four years to start my real estate investment business. Early in 1957 I met Sara Clark, a nursing student at St. Francis Hospital nursing school.

It may not have been love at first sight, but let's say I was very attracted to Sara. I used to go down to a boarding house once a day and eat lunch. I would go over there on Sunday to eat dinner.

Her boyfriend was the son of the lady who ran the boarding house. I went to the boarding house on Easter Sunday, 1957. She was there with her boyfriend. She was wearing sunshine yellow. Then I saw her a couple more times.

Then I went back in August and she was there by herself one Sunday.

She was just visiting what appeared to be her future mother-in-law, because her boyfriend wasn't there. I talked to her a little bit. She asked me for a ride downtown to the movies. I asked her if I could go to the movies with her. We went to see a show in the early afternoon. We rode out after that to Folly Beach, walking up and down the beach a little bit, watching the waves.

We came back and I asked her for a date after that. She was busy one or two days after that. We went out next on Wednesday. After that, we went out about every day for the next year.

About three months later, I asked her to marry me.

When I met her, she was already a Christian. It was about three years after I got saved.

We dated for one year from August of 1957 and we were married, after Sara graduated in August 1958, at St. Anthony's Catholic Church in Florence. This was the closest church to Marion, South Carolina, which was her home. Since we both lived in Charleston, we were given instructions by Father Stirker at the Cathedral. After we were married Sara worked as a RN at St. Francis until our first son was born in August of 1959.

In August of 1960, we moved back to Baltimore, Maryland for ten years. I worked in the legal profession for that period of time. In Baltimore, I acquired a Bible and read and studied it, many hours, days, months and years. Many Saturdays I studied the Bible all day long. We always attended the Catholic Church on Sundays.

As time went on we had four sons. Most of my working time I spent in the Baltimore County Courthouse in Towson, Maryland. I had a real estate title business and I did real estate titles work for a number of law firms and title guarantee companies.

I was very interested in political elections both local and national. When I was in law school I belonged to a political organization entitled Young Democrats of Students of Law. Joe Tidings was president of that organization when I belonged to it. His father was Senator Tidings of Maryland, one of the very well known senators at that time.

I thought that I had my life quite well planned. Since I was late getting started in college, this was the plan that I had for my life.

1. Age twenty to age forty would be education and research years and years to start my business.

2. Age forty to age sixty would be the business years. I would promote the business and get myself financially secure.

3. Age sixty to age eighty, I would either be in politics or work for the Lord.

In the years between 1960 and 1970 when we lived in Baltimore I had a real estate investment business in Charleston and a real estate title business for lawyers in Baltimore. For the last eight of those years, once a month we drove to Charleston, 550 miles each way, and stayed two and a half days there. We did this to keep the business going.

I asked the Lord what His will for my life was and in which of those places should I live permanently. So one day in 1968, the Lord spoke to me and said, "Pick up your family and move back to Charleston." I immediately said, "Okay, Lord," but I will need some extra money above and beyond my regular income to make the move.

Within about a year's time we were able to acquire a property in Charleston with no money down and sell it for a profit of $17,500. The Lord had answered my short prayer in a marvelous way. He loves to do that for His children. When he heals and when he answers prayer He gets the glory, the honor, and the praise. He loves to do that because He dwells in the praise of His people.

In August of 1970, we moved back to Charleston. Very shortly, through answered prayer, the Lord put me in the real estate investment business full time. In less than a year He provided another very fine investment property. This was when our youngest son Daniel O'Connell was only three. The other three boys, of the ages seven, nine, and eleven years old, went to the Cathedral school.

A MAN CALLED GEORGE

God spoke to me!

Starting in 1948 and lasting for twenty years until 1968, something happened in my life that seemed a bit unusual. In 1948, when Harry Truman ran for reelection I knew in my mind that he would win the election. I did not know how I knew, but I knew positively that he would. I also felt impressed to let someone know, but I did not know how I should do this, so the only thing that came to mind was that I will put up a bet with someone that this would happen. I bet five dollars that Harry Truman would win. It was a very close election and even one Chicago paper came out with a headline that Truman had lost the election.

Well this continued to happen in 1952 and 1956 with President Eisenhower, 1960 with Kennedy, with Johnson in 1964 and with Richard Nixon in 1968 and 1972. Also these were the years that the Holy Spirit had led me to fast more than ten full days each year. They were also the years when I spent much time studying the word of God. The only teacher that I had during that time was the Holy Spirit.

At that particular time in my life it came to my mind that Nixon was going to be the next president of the United States. These were times when I was in law school. This knowledge was coming from the Holy Spirit.

The Lord continued to show me about this. Of course it is for the purpose of ministering to the people in a better way---the word of knowledge. The Lord will show you things about this person, if you will pray. He will show you his need and how you can help him. This is a ministry gift. It is for the benefit of the church. It is not for the benefit of the person who has this knowledge. Jesus had this gift of knowledge. This is a gift of God for an individual who is praying and ministering and helping other people.

My sister Caroline lived in Alameda, California with her husband and five children. In March of 1968, I received a letter from her, telling me of some domestic relations problems she was having. On the 31st of March, I prayed before bed. I said Lord if there is anything I can do to help Caroline, please let me know.

At approximately 4 a.m., I woke up to a loud voice speaking to me. I sat up in bed and heard four distinctly different statements from the Lord. I quote the exact words He spoke: 1. "Richard Nixon shall be the next president of the United States. The assassination of President John F. Kennedy was the will of Almighty God. The second coming of Jesus Christ shall be within a period of time that will be ten years and twenty years from now." (And this Second Coming is for a particular person.)

The fourth item that He talked about was something that would be happening to me, and already has happened in the situation where I knew which candidate for the presidency would be elected.

It is the gift of the word of knowledge and it is for the benefit of the Body of Christ and it is set out in the

Bible. In I Corinthians 12:8 concerning this fourth item, He said, "You shall know (some things) that shall happen before they happen." When he stopped speaking to me, and without thinking about it, I heard my voice say Lord if that is you speaking to me, give me a sign. I had not had that experience before, as I was speaking under the anointing of the Lord from my spirit, and not from my mind.

As soon as I said that I started crying and I could not stop. My wife Sara said that this lasted for about forty-five minutes. I had never cried since I was a child because I always thought men do not cry. I did not want Sara to see me cry so I tried to be quiet. Sara woke up anyway because I could not stop crying. She asked what the matter was. I told her that the Lord was talking to me, then I told her what he said.

As the days went on, I tried to make sense out of the incident. I did not know that God spoke to people like that in these days. I had not heard of it. His voice sounded loud and audible to me. Within a couple of weeks or so the Lord spoke to me again in a quiet voice. He told me to write a letter to Richard Nixon and tell him that he would be elected president. I was to say that unless he would pick out three ministers of the Gospel and use them as advisors to him in his presidency, he would have great trouble in his administration.

Well, I had never heard of anything like the Lord speaking to a person and telling him to do something like this, except in the Bible, so I just let it go. More particularly, I had not heard anything like this in my church where my family and I attended regularly.

Another week or two went by and I became ill.

I went to the doctor, and he said that I had some symptoms of the mumps, but for some reason he said he did not think that I had the mumps. He asked me to go home and rest for a couple of days. When I got home Sara, knowing what to do, persuaded me to go to bed. When I went to bed the Lord spoke to me a second time and told me again to write the letter to Richard Nixon. Another unusual thing was the fact that I had his address in New York City, which is hard to acquire. I wrote the letter and mailed it, then soon thereafter I was totally well again. I did not expect to hear from him, and I did not.

The next thing that was on my mind was the Lord's words about the second coming of Jesus Christ. At first I thought about the great second coming of the Lord Jesus back to the earth, but the Bible tells us that no man knows the day or the hour of this great event. It seemed to me more like the coming of the lord for a specific individual.

For a while, I thought maybe the Lord was telling me that my time here on earth would be up before the twenty years was up. I asked the Lord many times to explain whose second coming he was talking about. I will explain about this later in my testimony because it was eighteen years before the Lord answered this question for me.

The Lord spoke to me at least five times in a loud audible voice, and a number of times in a softer voice. It was a bit later that same year of 1968 when the Holy Spirit spoke to me the third time in a loud voice. That day as I was walking across my living room at 1216 Sherwood Avenue in Baltimore, the Lord said to me, "There are many people in your church that are not saved." I stopped and closed my eyes and said, "Lord how could that be possible?

With all the colleges, universities, and institutions of higher learning that are within the auspices of the church, how could that be possible?"

I just could not grasp what the Lord had said that moment. At that point in time I could not understand that. I had thought up until that time that if you were a member of the church, you were saved. And if you confessed your sins and were forgiven that you would go to heaven. This statement that the Lord spoke to me that there were many people who were church members but they were not saved, gradually I started to understand as the Holy Spirit taught me and showed me about salvation.

VISIONS

In 1976, I read a book entitled *I Believe in Visions* by Rev. Kenneth Hagin. It was about his six major visions of Jesus Christ. "As I was in my hospital room, I heard footsteps coming down the corridor toward me. I looked to the door to see who it was because it was only 6:30 a.m., too early for visitors. Someone dressed in white came through the door and at first I thought it was a nurse. Then I looked closer, and I saw it was Jesus. It seemed as if my hair stood on end and goose bumps popped out all over my body and I couldn't say a word. This visit lasted nearly an hour and a half." Rev. Hagin told about these visits from Jesus in his book. Jesus told him many things about the Bible and his ministry and he told him to teach his people faith.

I was so fascinated by the book that I wanted to meet Rev. Hagin. When I heard that he was one of the speakers at the 1976 Word Convention of Full Gospel in Miami, my wife and I decided to go. We have heard him speak since then, and we have read many of his books. Today there are more than 20,000 graduates of Kenneth Hagin Ministries preaching the word around the world.

I have seen and read in the scriptures where others have had visions from God that God has given. I have heard so much about visions from the scriptures and from people who walk with the Lord that I believe in visions.

GOD SPEAKS TODAY

I guarantee He speaks today. He spoke to me many times, at least five major times in an audible voice. Many times He spoke in a soft voice. He has helped me many times in business. For instance, I am in the real estate investment business; I saw a building that I liked and I wanted to buy this building, so I asked the Lord, "Should I buy the building?" I wanted Him to tell me yes or no. In the meantime, I went up to the building and I prayed over it and I anointed it. Lord, hold this building for me until you tell me whether I should buy it or not. It was a long period of time before He answered me, but about nine months later, I was at breakfast one morning around 9 a.m., and the Lord answered that question to me, "My son, don't buy that building." I didn't know why or anything like that.

Immediately, I went back to the building and said, "Lord, I release this building for sale on the market." Within two weeks, the building sold. Someone else bought the building. Then I watched very closely. A doctor, who was in the Navy, bought the building. He was going to renovate the building and make his home out of it. The building was in such bad shape on the upper floors. The walls had about 15 sheets of wallpaper over the top of each other. When they tore that off, the bare walls were in terrible shape. A man spent $50,000 but could not get the building into shape good enough to live in. So the Lord was showing me that the investment would not have been a good one for me.

YOU CAN HEAR FROM GOD!

You can hear from the Lord when you become obedient to the Lord. The greatest miracle that there is, is the miracle of salvation. When we become saved, it is like putting on a coat, a coat of righteousness of Jesus Christ. We come closer to Him. Then we want to know Him better. As we come into the knowledge of Jesus Christ we come into salvation, where we have a greater desire to read His Word and study His Word and know about Him and to know Him personally.

As we read the Word of God and study the Word of God, that is the way we listen to God. The Bible is God's Word. As we get to know Him, just as in the Old Testament when it says Moses spent 40 years on the back side of the desert in preparation for the ministry that God had him to do, to lead the children of Israel out of captivity. As we spend time with the Lord we get to know Him better and better. After I had spent about eight years in my spare time reading the Bible every day, I came to know God much better than before.

When you do that, you believe Him and you trust Him, you open up to Him. You reach a certain place, a certain spiritual level in your life, and then you are able to hear God talk to you. After you study and read the Bible and spend time with the Lord regularly and daily for eight years. I was eight years in preparation.

He will do that for you; for anyone who loves Him and spends time with Him. He will speak to you. He is no respecter of persons. What He did for me, He will do for you. He will talk to you after you get to know Him and have that personal relationship with Him; after you have spent time in the Word with Him.

The more time you spend with Him, there is no quick way to do that; you have to KNOW Him and trust Him. You have to believe in Him and be obedient to His Word. Those are the ingredients to hear from Him. That is the only way hearing from the Holy Spirit comes about.

Power of the Holy Spirit

I had not seen Howard and Grace Chatham for fifteen years, since they moved from Baltimore in 1955 to Andrews, North Carolina, in the mountains where they retired. They had not met my wife or children, so in June of 1973, we went to Andrews to see them for a couple of days.

Chatham said, "You know, Duggan, since we last saw you both Grace and I have been baptized in the Holy Spirit." I asked, "Chatham, what is that?" I had never heard of that. He said, "When you get back to Charleston, look up the Full Gospel Business Men's Fellowship, International. They will tell you what it is." When we came back, I missed the July meeting, but I saw the advertisement for the August meeting in the paper. I went to this meeting.

It was a Friday night once a month with a speaker and a prayer breakfast, as well as Bible studies every Saturday morning. In the morning I went to the prayer breakfast. It was so different from any group that I had been around. They read the Bible and talked about it, and the Lord talked to these people like he had been talking to me. I had never met anyone before that the Lord had spoken to. In our church I had never met anyone whom the

Lord had spoken to. I was so happy that for the next three months all I could do was to sit through these breakfasts and weep with joy.

I was invited to their business meetings that they had once a month at the home of one of the members. I will never forget how long they prayed at these business meetings. They usually prayed for at least one full hour. I said to myself, "Lord, when are they ever going to stop praying?" Well, when they prayed for an hour or so they could usually finish the business part in about twenty minutes, so I knew that the Lord must have been there.

When they had their annual meeting in December, I was nominated for vice president of the chapter. I said, "I can't be an officer because I do not have the baptism in the Holy Spirit." The chapter president proclaimed, "We will take care of that. Come over and sit in this chair!" They led me in a prayer for me to receive the Baptism in the Holy Spirit.

Some two weeks later, at home beside my bed, the evidence came forth. I started speaking a foreign language that I did not know or understand. I found out shortly that I could start or stop praying in tongues anytime that I wanted. It was very uplifting. Also at a time when you were tired or burdened, praying in tongues was very refreshing and it just moved burdens and heaviness away from you.

It made praying much easier than before. It was no longer a chore like it had been. Everyone I saw I wanted to pray for. I was much bolder than before. Before this I could not speak in public. In college I even had a difficult time reading from a book in front of the class. Now a short while after the Baptism in the Holy Spirit, I could stand up and speak in front of people with ease, and this did not bother me at all.

When I told Sara what had happened to me, she said she wanted to receive this gift too. In January she came to a breakfast meeting. At the meeting they prayed for her to receive the baptism of the Holy Spirit. Sara spoke in tongues immediately, and this made a big difference in her life, because she used to have a temper. Previously, if she would get angry, or if there was a difference between us, she usually took several days to get over it. After she received the baptism of the Holy Spirit with the evidence of speaking in tongues as in Acts 2:4, it only took her five minutes to get over being angry or upset.

The Bible tells us in Acts 2:4 that on the day of Pentecost, the 120 were all filled with the Holy Spirit, and they spoke in other tongues as the Spirit gave them utterance. That is how you know that you have the baptism of the Holy Spirit, because you speak in unknown tongues.

Three of our four sons are baptized in the Holy Spirit. Most stayed with the Lord even through high school and college. The second and third oldest Patrick and James received the baptism when they were in about the eighth grade. We took them to the Full Gospel breakfasts, Bible studies, and youth meetings at the World Convention of the FGBMFI.

When Daniel, our youngest son, was ten years old we took him to the Full Gospel World Convention in Chicago. At the youth meeting, Daniel accepted an invitation to receive salvation and the baptism in the Holy Spirit. A friend of ours saw tears streaming down Daniel's face as he walked forward, under conviction of his sins.

When he came back to his seat, he was speaking in a new prayer language.

All four of our sons were baptized in water, confirmed, and active in our church. It was a joy to have children who walked with the Lord through their youthful years of high school and college.

Acts 2:4 says, "And they were all filled with the Holy Spirit and began to speak in foreign tongues, even as the Holy Spirit prompted them to speak." This was two thousand years ago when the church started on the day of Pentecost. As the years went by the experience died out in the church.

At the turn of the century about 1890 to 1900, an unusual thing started happening in the Kansas City area and on west to Los Angeles on Azuza Street. Many Bible studies started popping up in homes and then they got so big, the people started meeting in old warehouses and larger buildings. Out of these movements, the Pentecostal church was born. In fifty years this Pentecostal church moved all the way around the world. I do not think we can call the Pentecostal church Protestant, because it was not in existence at the time of the Reformation in Europe. It seems to be a third branch of the church.

In 1949 there was a man by the name of David Du Plessis who moved from South Africa to the U.S. He called himself a classical Pentecostalist. "Brother David" was what we called him. He traveled quite extensively back and forth, mostly to Europe and the U.S., and became very well known. He wrote a number of books, but the best known were *The Spirit Bade Me Go* and *Mr. Pentecost*. He was dubbed Mr. Pentecost by Pope John Paul.

Acts 2:4 is a life-changing scripture. You receive genuine power when you receive the Holy Spirit, whenever you ask the Holy Spirit to come into your life. You get what the scriptures call "the Baptism in the Holy Spirit." Jesus Christ is the baptizer. You ask Him to fill you with the Holy Spirit as a powerful change. In the Book of Acts, Jesus told His followers not to go out and preach until they were endued with power. That is when we are endued with the power of the Holy Spirit. That is where the ministry gifts come into our lives, when we ask for that power.

You and I do not possess the power to defeat the enemy, without the Holy Spirit. We have the power over the enemy. With these gifts and the power of the Holy Ghost, it says the scriptures tell us that after salvation we have a measure of the Holy Spirit. But when we receive the Pentecostal blessing, as in Acts 2:4, while we are filled with the Holy Spirit, then we are endued with power from on high. We have a power when the enemy, Satan, is acting up against us; we have the power to overcome that situation.

We have the power to cast out demons. We have the spiritual power from on high that we receive from the Lord Jesus Christ to really minister and to help others see through the gifts of the Holy Spirit, to really see through the false front that the enemy puts on many times. The activities of Satan when he comes like an angel of light, the scriptures tell us, to mislead us, to misguide us, to fool us. But with this power, we can truly work and do the work of the Lord.

There is no other way that we can truly work, because if Jesus was given this power when the Holy Spirit came upon Him, when He was on the earth, in His ministry, how much more do we need that power today?

Jesus said, "Don't go out and try to minister until you are endued with the power from on high, like in Acts 2:4, throughout the book of Acts."

The Baptism in the Holy Spirit made a very distinct difference in my life. I was a very shy person. For the first time, when the power of the Lord came upon me through the Baptism in the Holy Spirit, I could stand up in front of people and speak and talk to them and explain the Word of God. I could tell them about the Word of God. I am not a preacher. I am a lay person, but I can give my testimony which showed how the power of God was used in my life, and other people could see it for the first time from my point of view.

Through salvation we receive a "measure" of the Holy Spirit. That is what the scripture says. We receive a measure of the Holy Spirit. There is a great difference in the measure of the spirit and through the Pentecostal experience, we are filled with the Holy Spirit. We only have a measure of flour in a container; it is not full. To me, that is what that is saying. If you really want to go out and work for the Lord, you need to be filled with the Holy Spirit. That is what the Word of God is saying.

A measure of the Holy Spirit means you are not FULL of the Holy Spirit, so you still lack the full power. The Holy Spirit helps you to overcome the power of the Enemy, the devil. For the gifts to operate fully in your life, so you can bring the un-churched in areas of the world unto salvation.

A MAN CALLED GEORGE

Is there any sick among you?

Healing and miracles ARE for us today! That is why Jesus came down on the earth and spent time, and selected His disciples and taught them and showed them as He walked each day with them in Jerusalem and in the Wilderness over there. No matter where we go, He taught that if you believe, by faith, that you can be healed. I totally believe in faith healing. God's Word says so in the Bible. God cannot lie. By those stripes on Jesus' back, we are healed. There are many other scriptures that show this truth in the Bible.

WE SHOULD PRAY FOR OTHERS

Go to the scriptures and we see the ministry that Jesus had. Jesus taught His disciples the same things that He did, He said that you can do. That was His main theme in the three-plus years He was on the earth in ministry. He took His disciples many places. They saw Him pray for many people. In Acts, He said that all power is given unto Me in heaven and in earth. He gave that spiritual power, the power of almighty God to ordinary people. In Acts 2:4, He told His disciples don't go out and preach. Stay here in Jerusalem until you receive the promise of the Father. That is what happened on the Day of Pentecost. There were 120 in the Upper Room. The power of God the Holy Spirit descended upon them; and they received the power of God.

Because the 120 were obedient they stayed there until they received the power of the Lord Jesus Christ. When they had the Pentecostal power, they received the Baptism in the Holy Spirit (the name of it in the Bible). That gave them the power to minister. There were nine gifts of the Holy Spirit which worked in their lives. As they were obedient to the Lord Jesus Christ, YOU can be obedient. YOU can go out and pray for people just as Jesus did. You can lay hands on them and pray for their healing, for their deliverance, and for their needs. God said that He would honor that. And He does when we are obedient to His Word. He said that obedience is better than sacrifice. When you walk with Him in obedience and you trust Him and you believe, you see the results when you pray.

HEALING OF GALL STONES

In 1970 I went to be examined by a doctor for abdominal pain. The doctor had x-rays made at St. Francis Hospital. He said I had gallstones that had to be surgically removed. He wanted to know what surgeon I wanted to use. I told him that I would let him know.

It came to my mind that I had been healed four times by miracles of healing. I believed the Lord would heal me if I asked him and had someone pray for me with the gift of healing. While I was waiting to find someone to pray for me I had to be careful what I ate so I did not have an attack of pain. Papaya juice was one of the few things that would relieve the pain. I had been working with the local chapter of Full Gospel Businessmen's Fellowship for a few months.

In the spring of 1974, we had a speaker who had the gift of healing in his ministry. We usually did not have our meetings in churches, but that spring we had three of our meetings in the Citadel Square Baptist Church. Our speaker gave an invitation for healing at the end of his testimony. Many people came for healing that night. The line of people went almost to the back of the church.

I stood beside the speaker and held the microphone as he prayed for each one. Every person in that line said the pain was gone or that they were healed. Some people were visibly healed. The last two people in the line had one leg that was shorter than the other. The Lord instantly healed both of them.

The speaker spoke at five or six other prayer meetings and places before he left Charleston but while he was here I asked him to pray for the healing of my gallstone condition. He prayed for me. And I thought that I was healed, but several weeks later I had another attack of pain and it always seemed to happen about 4 a.m. in the morning. I got up to drink papaya juice for relief. Medication did not help the pain that I had.

I went on for a while longer, occasionally with the papaya juice at 4 a.m. in the morning. There I was, in my living room at 4 a.m. in the morning with a glass of papaya juice in my left hand. I couldn't believe that the Lord did not heal me. I shook my fist towards heaven and said, "Lord why didn't you heal me?" All the other times that I had been prayed for something, I was healed. But this was the first time I was not healed when I was prayed for.

To my surprise He spoke back to me in a bit of a rough voice, like I spoke to Him and said, "You eat too much." Then I said, "Well, what about my wife?" The Lord spoke again and said in the most beautiful, loving voice that I have ever heard, "Your wife is her own person. You cannot tell her what to do. When you get your eating habits under control, I am going to heal you!"

That was the end of the conversation at that time.

During the next year (another year went by before I was healed), a couple of times I came out and drank papaya juice again. The Lord spoke to me, "Wake your wife and have her pray for you." So I woke Sara up and I told her, "Sara, the Lord said if you will pray for me, He will heal me." She did. She put her hand on my shoulder and said, "Be healed in Jesus' name!"

The pain left me, just like that. I was totally healed from gallstones.

I knew that I was healed because in a week or two I tried the foods that I could not eat before, especially ice cream and roast beef. I could eat all of them without pain. For a long time I had wanted to pray for people and have God heal them. In December of 1973, I had received the baptism in the Holy Spirit and Sara had received it in January of 1974.

About this same time a man came up to me at our prayer breakfast and told me that one of his legs was longer than the other. He asked if I would pray for healing in his leg. I was surprised that he asked me as I had not prayed for anyone's healing before. I asked another person whom I knew to come pray with me for him. I didn't give it any thought at that particular time. I was just ready to pray for anyone's healing.

We asked him to sit down in a chair and hold his legs straight out. With his legs together you could see that one was about five eighths of an inch shorter than the other. We prayed for him right there. With just a few words I said, "Heavenly Father, I ask you to heal this man's leg in Jesus' name." As soon as I said those words his leg started growing out. It started moving out. It scared me at first because it grew out longer than the other leg. Then it went back and evened up with it as a perfect match.

This was the beginning of my praying for healing of others.

I had always had a desire ever since I had the salvation experience to pray for others and have God heal them. I was just elated about this, that the Lord had healed this man's leg.

At this time our children were growing up and we found out that we could pray for them for all the things that children get. The Lord most always healed them.

SARA PRAYS FOR OTHERS

My wife Sara was a registered nurse at St. Francis Hospital. She had been witnessing to another nurse who spent most of her time outside of work in bars because of a drinking problem. She was Catholic but she went to church very little. On January 10, 1975, our Full Gospel chapter had its monthly meeting in the Francis Marion Hotel. We had a Catholic speaker that month and a lot of Catholic people came to the meeting. After the speaker gave his testimony he invited people to come to the front to receive salvation or the baptism in the Holy Spirit. This nurse came up and prayed the sinner's prayer. She received salvation.

After that she prayed to receive the Baptism in the Holy Spirit, which she received. We knew she received this gift because she left praying in tongues. We also knew that she received her salvation because a person can't speak in tongues unless she is saved.

About three weeks later, on the fifth day of February, I went to Beaufort to my cousin's funeral. When I got home at 5 p.m., the children told me Sara had gone to this nurse's apartment because something had happened. I immediately felt a strong leading of the Holy Spirit to go to the apartment where Sara had gone. When I got to her apartment there were two other women there and the nurse was lying in her bed. When the bed moved she flinched with pain. They told me that she fell down the stairs and injured her back going to the second floor.

My wife asked me to pray for the Lord to heal her back. Sara took my hand and placed it on the woman's back. As I prayed the Holy Spirit spoke to me in an audible voice and said, "Cast out the demons." At that point I straightened up and had to think what to do. I had only been taught how to cast out demons from the Bible but I had not done it before this time myself.

It was a tense moment and I began to perspire, but I knew that God was in control and that he had the power to cast the demons out. My first thoughts were that I needed to get the Catholic priests from the Cathedral parish, but the Holy Spirit answered even that thought, so I decided I had just better get busy and get the job done. I knew the women could not hear the Holy Spirit as He spoke to me, even though it sounded audible to me, so I told them that the woman had demons and we had to cast them out. In some churches they call this procedure exorcism, but since I studied it from the Bible, I usually use biblical terminology.

I then asked one of the women to open the Bible to the gospel of John and read God's Word out loud. When she read the Word, I commanded the demons to come out in Jesus' name. The nurse passed out as in a fainting spell. The demons hollered out of her in a loud voice, "Who are you? If you don't let us alone we will hurt her and we are going to kill her." (Everyone in the room could hear the demons hollering. It was not like the voice of the Holy Spirit.)

I said, "Shut up and be quiet. I command you to come out in Jesus' name." Her mouth opened as if she was going to throw up; and the first demon or group of demons came out. I commanded them to come out a second time and the same thing happened. I commanded them a third time to come out and a third one or third group came out. Her eyes opened in a few moments, and she said thank you Jesus. She picked up her Bible and held it to her bosom. She was set free. It was about 6 p.m. when she went to sleep.

She slept all night, and until 3 p.m. the next afternoon. She had been very fearful of the dark and consequently, for a number of years, she always slept with her lights on. Sara told me that she only slept for about four hours a night, so she brought her to our home to sleep on our sofa every few days for several weeks until she got back to normal. The Lord also healed her back injury that afternoon. When she went to the V.A. Hospital for a check up about three weeks after that, they x-rayed her back. The x-rays showed that the arthritis in that area of her back was also healed.

A great change came about in her life. Fifteen days after she received salvation and the baptism of the Holy Spirit, she was set free from demonic possession. Right after this she started attending her church in Charleston, South Carolina on a regular basis until this day, more than twenty years later. Shortly after she was saved she took a Bible correspondence course from the Rhema Bible Training Center in Tulsa, Oklahoma. Today she has a street ministry on the streets of Charleston.

MY SISTER CAROLINE

My sister Caroline who lived in Alameda, California stopped going to church most of the time. She just dropped out and seemed to have no interest in the Lord or church anymore. In 1976 my mother died and my sister and I both went to the funeral in Florida. My other brother John, who lived in Florida, had gone out after the funeral with Caroline to a restaurant. We both felt that she did not have a salvation experience, even though we grew up in the church.

John talked to Caroline and witnessed to her about salvation that evening. When they came home, I explained salvation to her as the Bible explains it. After that she indicated that she would like to be sure that she was saved. So that evening, I led my sister Caroline in the sinner's prayer, or prayer of faith. She asked Jesus to come into her heart and take over her life. She had emphysema so I also prayed for healing. She also prayed for the Baptism of the Holy Spirit.

The next day there was a big change in her life. Her emphysema was so much better that she forgot to take her medicine.   She did not need the medicine because she had no problem breathing. As she was flying back to California a few days later, she received her prayer language and started to speak in tongues on the plane. She started attending church on a regular basis. She was just different than before. She was much more enthusiastic about spiritual things.

In 1978 we visited Caroline at her home in California. She was still healed of the emphysema. In 1980 we met her again in Los Angeles at the World Convention of Full Gospel. She was still healed at that time. However, in 1986 the emphysema condition came back to her. She was seriously ill in the hospital.

If we are not strong in the Lord and have once had a disease Satan will try to put it back on us. It helps to be strong in the Word. The power of God is in the Word of God and in the name of Jesus. And we should know how to use it. Even Jesus used the Word three times to command Satan to leave him and stop tempting him.

Caroline moved back to Florida and as a result of the emphysema, she died in the hospital. Her funeral was on April 1, 1986. At the moment I did not realize what had happened exactly eighteen years before on the same day. In the second chapter of this book I mentioned that the first time that the Lord spoke to me in an audible voice was on April 1, 1968.

One of the things that He said to me was that the Second Coming of Jesus Christ shall be within a period of time, ten years and twenty years from now. It was not clear to me whose Second Coming the Lord was speaking about, so in August of 1986, I was standing in my bathroom and I asked the Lord again, "Lord, whose second coming were you talking about?"

Then he spoke to me and said, "Whom did you pray for the night I spoke to you?" I suddenly realized that it was my sister Caroline whom the Lord was talking about, eighteen years before. His words now meant even more than they did then, for he said the Second Coming of Jesus, which meant he took her up to heaven with him. The funeral was on the same day eighteen years later from the time when the Lord first spoke to me in an audible voice. Hallelula!

HEALING

On another trip to Florida there was a charismatic conference at St. Leo's Abbey, in Dade City, about three miles from where I grew up, that we attended for several days. The priests from the abbey pastored several of the rural churches in the area, including St. Joseph's where I attended as a boy. Two of the speakers were Bill Basansky and Father Francis McNutt.

I knew many of the people at the conference from two Catholic parishes in the area. For many of them it was their first exposure to faith healing and the charismatic events in a conference setting. In one long session that lasted at least three hours, Father McNutt was teaching on faith healing. He had three persons come up for prayer; all three were healed. One lady had arthritis in her arms that kept her from being able to raise them. He prayed for her, and she could raise her arms part of the way. He prayed for her a second time, and she could raise them higher. After a third prayer, she could raise her arms somewhat above her shoulders. Then he had the people pray for healing with each other.

Francis McNutt lives in Jacksonville, Florida, and he still has a healing ministry. We took my brother Dan to this conference with us. It was his first time to visit a charismatic event. Dan was not saved yet at this time. He prayed the sinner's prayer earlier that year when my sister received salvation, but there was no change in his life. He went to church regularly but it was out of a sense of duty. Eight years later he went to an evangelistic meeting and came back changed. He had excitement about the things of the Lord, and he bought a Bible that he still uses every day.

Sometime later I asked him about the change in his life. I said, "Dan, you prayed the sinner's prayer the same night that Caroline did and she was saved, but there was no change in you; what happened to you?" He then told me that he did not understand what I was talking about. The prayer had no meaning to him, so he got nothing out of it.

Bill Basansky and his family came out of Russia right after World War II. Somehow they got to America. He was a Russian communist when he got here. Then he was in an accident here and became paralyzed from the waist down. Someone took him to a Kathryn Kuhlman meeting where he was instantly healed and saved. For five years after that he taught Russian at Oral Roberts University.

We knew him as he had been to Charleston and was one of our speakers at the Eastern Regional Full Gospel Convention in Myrtle Beach. He prayed for healing. Almost everyone asked him for prayer, then they went "down" under the power of the Lord. At the St. Leo Conference my brother was the only person left in his seat. He watched everyone move, but he wasn't moving.

At the end Bill invited people to receive the Baptism in the Holy Spirit, and a very large group came. Sara and I helped him minister to the group. They asked Jesus to baptize them in the Holy Spirit as in Acts 2:4. As I went from person to person, everyone that I heard spoke in tongues.

When Father McNutt prayed for healing at the end of his teaching, a lady who was demon-possessed asked for prayer. He started to pray for her and she quickly passed out. Demons started yelling and cursing out of her in very foul language. It took at least forty-five minutes or longer before she was set free.

FINGER HEALED

One afternoon after my painter left work for the day I went in the storeroom and saw that he had left a can of paint open. I picked up the lid and a heavy chisel with burs on the end. When I went to tap the lid shut I hit my thumbnail with one of the steel burs on the chisel and busted a hole through the center of my thumbnail a quarter of an inch wide and long, pushing part of the thumbnail down into the flesh. I just shook my hand, without saying anything negative, but thinking how bad that thumb could be.

Since I needed building material for the next day, I got in my car and drove across the old Ashley River Bridge. The Lord spoke in such an audible voice that he could have been sitting next to me. He said four words, "Pray for your finger." I immediately put both of my thumbs up to my mouth with my elbows on the steering wheel, and said, "Finger, be healed in Jesus' name." Then I promptly put my hands back on the steering wheel and forgot about it.

Not until the next morning when getting out of bed did I think about it again. I said, "Oh, my finger." I looked at it and it was totally healed. It had turned purple but even that was gone, all except a small moon shaped sliver of purple in the center of the thumbnail.

Isn't God wonderful?

First, He reminded me to pray for my own finger, and then He healed it. He really does love us and care about us, even with something as small as a finger. God can do what He said He can do in His Word. In order for my finger to be healed right away by a miracle, someone had to pray for the healing. Jesus said, "And I tell you, ask and you will receive; seek and you will find; knock and the door will be opened to you." (Luke 11:9)

In James 5:14-15 the text says, "Is anyone among you sick? He should summon the presbyters of the church, and they should pray over him and anoint him with oil in the name of the Lord. And the prayer of faith will save the sick person, and the Lord will raise him up. If he has committed any sins, he will be forgiven."

Jesus said many times that it is by our faith that we are healed. Hebrews 11:1 says, "Faith is the realization of what is hoped for and evidence of things not seen." In another version, the word now, at the beginning of Hebrews 11:1 means that faith is always in the present tense. You must believe it now before you are healed, then you will be healed. On the other side, the opposite of faith is doubt and unbelief. We must overcome this doubt and unbelief to become healed.

When I prayed for my thumb I prayed out loud.

Why did I do this? I needed to believe in my mind and in my inner person, my spirit, so when I said finger be healed in Jesus' name, those words went out into the air. They came in my ears and lodged in my spirit, and caused both my mind and my spirit to believe for the miracle. It is like baking a cake. All of the ingredients are important. It is the same with receiving your miracle with prayer. All of these items are important ingredients. It helps to know that it is always God's will for us to be healed, and we know this because He says so in His Word.

Hebrews 11:6 says, "But without faith it is impossible to please him, for anyone who approaches God must believe that he exists and that he rewards those who seek him. If we are spiritually weak and we need more faith, we need to overcome doubt and unbelief in our life." Romans 10:17 explains how to do that. It says, "Thus faith comes from what is heard, and what is heard comes through the word of Christ." Another translation says, "So then faith comes by hearing; and hearing by the Word of God." The more we hear God's Word the stronger our faith becomes, and the more our faith increases.

John 15:7-8 is another helpful passage about the Word and God's work. It says, "If you remain in me and my words remain in you, ask for whatever you want and it will be done for you. By this is my Father glorified, that you bear much fruit and become my disciples."

When I said finger be healed in Jesus' name, the mention of Jesus' name released the power of Jesus upon my finger. If I had done everything required of me by the Word, which apparently I had done in this case, the presence of God and the anointing of God came forth and the miracle of healing took place.

A MAN CALLED GEORGE

"Many people in your church are not saved!"

God spoke to me, "Many people in your church are not saved!" That was the third time that the Lord spoke to me in an audible voice. This was in 1968. My wife and I were living in Baltimore, Maryland. I walked across the living room. I was in the middle of the living room under the chandelier when the Lord spoke to me.

He said, "My son, there are many people in your church, the Roman Catholic Church, that are not saved." I said, right away, just like I was talking to Him, "Lord, how is that possible? With all the colleges and universities and institutions of higher learning that are under the auspices of the church?" I had never thought of that before. I had always thought that people who were in church and going to church, I always thought of them as being saved. It was a new idea to me. It kind of startled me at first.

But I started thinking about what God said. Then it was about four years after that, I was in some of the charismatic and FGBMFI meetings. I would see them praying for people. They would have the altar calls. They were praying for salvation, usually. It just took a period of time to get used to this idea and start to understand and find out in the scriptures how people actually got saved or born again, as it says in John chapter 3, when Jesus was talking to Nicodemus. As I saw this happen, meeting after meeting after meeting, I saw the leaders call people up to raise up their hands and if they had never prayed the sinner's prayer and they wanted salvation. I saw it happening. The Lord was speaking to me in a quiet voice, leading me in different places during that period of time.

The first people I actually prayed for were my sister and my brother at my mother's funeral; and I saw a great difference in their lives. As I saw this happen in many different charismatic meetings, and as I read the scriptures, I came to understand the scriptures I read. It showed me how people got saved. The Holy Spirit was emphasizing this and leading me. That is actually how this happened in my life.

HOLY SPIRIT POURED OUT
ON ALL FLESH

We had a Hollywood movie star who was a Christian come to Charleston and speak at our Full Gospel Chapter monthly meeting. He was an actor on the weekly television show called "Highway 66." While he was in Charleston, we were able to have him speak to the students at Bishop England Catholic High School. Some of the classes were let out, and the students came to the auditorium to hear this speaker give his testimony. After his testimony, he talked to the students about salvation, and what they needed to do to be saved.

In John 3: 5-6 Jesus said, "Jesus answered, Amen, Amen, I say to you, no one can enter the kingdom of God without being born of water and spirit. What is born of flesh is flesh and what is born of spirit is spirit." After this the speaker prayed for the students and the meeting was over.

A bit later, the Holy Spirit indicated to me that less than 49 percent of the students in these high schools were saved when they graduated. The Holy Spirit gave me a mental picture of a spiritual barometer. The Holy Spirit was saying that each individual person is very unique. They look different. Each has distinctive fingerprints and a different DNA. The Lord has given each one of us a ministry for our life's work, which is different.

Also, each one of us has a different spiritual level, as we have different academic levels, to go along with our uniqueness and preciousness as the way God sees us. On the spiritual barometer the Lord said that 212 degrees represents the level of salvation, which is the temperature of boiling water. The spiritual level of the Baptism in the Holy Spirit is 315 degrees, which is the temperature of super-heated steam that is used to turn steam turbines on large ocean going vessels. The Holy Spirit said to me that our spiritual level or spiritual understanding cannot go above 212 degrees unless and until we have the born again experience, also called conversion or salvation.

Somehow or other, we only see darkly, we do not see as clearly in our spiritual understanding about spiritual things as we will see when we have salvation. This is especially true when we are reading, studying, and trying to understand the Bible, because the Bible is a spiritual book. Salvation gets us into heaven, but we need the power (Acts 2:4) in our lives for ministry. We need the Holy Spirit power, so we will have the gifts of the Holy Spirit in operation. This helps to keep us out of temptation and enables us to minister in power for the Lord.

We must be saved before we can receive the Baptism in the Holy Spirit as in Acts 2:4. Please note that the Word of God says in Matthew 3:11, Mark 1:8, Luke 3:11, John 1:33, and John 1:4 that Jesus Christ is the Baptizer in the Holy Spirit. The Word says that with salvation we have a *measure* of the Holy Spirit, but with the Baptism of the Holy Spirit we are *filled* with the Holy Spirit; that is the difference.

STATISTICAL ANALYSIS

One of the latest George Barna annual surveys published in *Charisma* magazine in July of 1997, page 17, on born again or saved Catholics, says that in 1995 only 39 percent of Catholic church members were saved. In 1997 the figure had moved up, stating that 43 percent of members were saved.

Ray Bullard lived in South Bend, Indiana and was a member of Calvary Temple Pentecostal Church. Over the years he was very active in his church, being a deacon and a Sunday school teacher. Ray was introduced to Full Gospel Business Men's Fellowship International when Demos Shakarian, the International president and founder, came to South Bend to speak. He liked what he heard from Demos so well that he later went to a convention in Denver, Colorado, became a member, and started a chapter in South Bend. A few years later he became president of the chapter and was excited to serve the Lord in that capacity.

At a later period of time when I met Ray Bullard, he was an International Director in the Fellowship, and I was a Chapter Vice President. I met him at one of our world conventions, in the delegates and international directors' business meeting. I had heard about Ray's testimony concerning some students from Notre Dame University in the January 1977 issue of *Voice* magazine. I wanted to confirm the story, personally, so I went after our business meeting and talked to Ray about the meeting that he had with the students.

This is that confirmed story. In March of 1967, he said, "I received a telephone call from someone at Notre Dame University." The speaker said, "I'm a Roman Catholic. There are nine of us on the Notre Dame campus who have been praying now for two weeks for a deeper experience. Will you help us?" Ray said, "I don't know if I'll be able to help, but let's have a prayer meeting and share some experiences."

At our next meeting, which was on March 13, 1967, about thirty men from a Pentecostal church and nine Roman Catholics from Notre Dame University were in attendance. It was exciting, but at the same time a little frightening, because I began to worry that I wouldn't have the right words for these intellectual professors, some of whom weren't shy about letting us know that they had an intellectual hang up. But I silently turned the meeting over to Christ and immediately a wonderful change took place.

The Spirit of the Lord came upon our prayer meeting and within minutes, it seemed that they all received the gift of tongues. I never saw such joy and happiness. They were hugging each other and the joy of the Lord was upon that place. It turned out to be one of the sweetest and most beautiful prayer meetings I've ever been involved in. I found out later that the nine men from Notre Dame had received the Baptism in the Holy Spirit by faith with the laying on of hands the week before at a prayer meeting on campus.

These men went back to the campus the next day and began to tell different ones about what had happened in our prayer meeting. One person from the group was named Bert Ghezzi. He told Father Edward O'Connor, who was head of the Theological Department of Notre Dame University for fifteen years, that the night before he had received the gift of tongues. Not only had he received, but practically everybody else in that room had received the gift, except Professor O'Connor. The very next Monday Professor O'Connor was at our home seeking the Baptism in the Holy Spirit, and I believe God really touched him at that time. He's been a real inspiration and help to our Full Gospel Business Men's Chapter as well as the Pentecostal group of believers at Notre Dame.

About three weeks after this the men at Notre Dame held their first annual Pentecostal conference. The conference lasted from Friday through Sunday afternoon. They called me Saturday to come over and help them, but I was busy with a Full Gospel Business Men's Fellowship meeting in Battle Creek, Michigan. As soon as I got home, however, I went over to the campus and found a tremendous group of young Catholic students seeking God. As we began to pray for them they began to receive the Holy Spirit, and I think that weekend between thirty and forty were filled.

Joel prophesied that "upon all flesh" the Lord would pour out of His Spirit in the last days (Joel 3:1&2 and in Acts 2:17-21). Father O'Connor knew this story, from its inception, better than anyone did. A short period of time after it happened, Father O'Connor shared the story at a

FGBMFI gathering and a brief version of it was published in the July-August 1967 issue of *Voice* magazine. Not only did this happen at Notre Dame, but within a few months the Lord was pouring out His Spirit upon all. This Pentecostal experience was being poured out for the first time on young lay persons at Notre Dame, and then about the same time at Wheaton College, St. Mary's College, Michigan State, Duquesne, and Iowa.

A MAN CALLED GEORGE

Breakthroughs in Life

Shortly after my salvation experience, Chatham gave me a book to read about fasting entitled *Because of Your Unbelief.* The author, Franklin Hall, was a student and specialist of fasting. Inside the front cover of the book was a testimony of a young sailor named Ken Cantrell, who was given the book, which he tried to throw away several times. It kept coming back to him each time, so he finally read the book. He was on the aircraft carrier Lake Champlain, which was in San Diego when he got the book, but after reading it he went on a total fast, eating nothing and drinking only water.

On the 17th day of his total fast, the ship was in the Mediterranean Sea and he and fifteen other sailors were in the catapult room under the flight deck when a fuel tank on an aircraft ruptured. It was being fueled on the flight deck, and high-octane fuel came through the ventilator into the catapult room and exploded into flames, and within moments the other fifteen sailors were dead.

But Ken Cantrell continued to walk through the fire unharmed, with the book in his pocket; the book fell out onto the red-hot deck and did not burn. His clothes did not burn and after about thirty minutes God spoke to him to open the hatch and go out, which he did. There were about two thousand witnesses to this incident and it was in some of the newspapers. Because of the seventeen-day fast, his life was saved, and he became a minister of the Gospel after that.

After I read the book, I was moved to go on a three-day fast. The results were powerful. The Lord led me to do a series of these fasts that were a total of ten days a year total fast, and this lasted for over twenty years. These fasts had a very positive and profound effect on my spiritual life.

Jesus' disciples were asking him a question about casting out a demon. A problem they were having in Matthew 17:19-20. He told them that they could not cast the demon out because of their unbelief, or lack of faith. "But this kind can be cast out only by prayer and fasting."

Several years after the Lord healed my back, I was being examined by a doctor for life insurance. The doctor told me that I had very severe high blood pressure, and could not even get life insurance. I went to another doctor who put me on medication and treatment for high blood pressure for awhile. In the winter of 1960-61, a Catholic Church in Baltimore was having a healing service. I went to the service and was prayed for and the next night I noticed that my blood pressure had gone down, and I was totally healed of that condition. I have not had any high blood pressure problem since.

In 1970 I was having pain in my right leg, especially after driving long distances in my automobile. I went to a healing evangelist meeting in Charleston and was prayed for and the pain in my right leg was healed as I was walking away from the meeting.

About 1974, I had severe pain in my left leg. The doctor could not find anything wrong with it. I made an appointment with a specialist who was out of town at the time and his waiting list was quite long. It was so bad that I used a crutch to walk with for several weeks. By this time my wife Sara and I had learned how to pray for our own healing. I went on a fast and we prayed for my leg and on the eighth day of a total fast (no food to eat, only water to drink on these fasts), the pain went out of my leg and it was totally healed.

In James 5:14 it says pray for the sick. Verse 15 says "and the prayer of faith will save the sick man, and the Lord will raise him up, and if he be in sins they shall be forgiven him."

I was persuaded to believe in fasting because I saw that fasting worked for me in many different ways. Fasting is just an every day practical way to keep me from getting overweight. That is not spiritual at all; that's just physical. It was very healthy for my body not to overeat and not to gain too much weight. The fasting that I did approximately 10-12 days a year for over 20 years kept me in good physical shape. It was hard for me to believe to start with that we could be addicted to food. By going on the fast that I went on, I broke the addiction of having to eat when I thought about food or smelled good food.

I could miss a breakfast. I could miss a meal at any time, without any problem whatsoever, when I broke the addiction through fasting. That helps you in everyday life. Maybe you are in a hurry sometime to do something very important. It is going to take you an hour to eat a meal. Then to realize that you do not have to take that time, it is a tremendous advantage sometime in your life, just a little thing like that.

You can always offer it up to the Lord. In the Bible, it even speaks about giving this food to somebody who needs it more who does not have very much.

I usually fasted in the wintertime. One of the reasons why I got into this fasting, I had prayed and had asked the Lord how I had a problem catching colds all the time. Anytime I got a sore throat, no matter what I did, I could not prevent myself from catching a cold. So I prayed about this. Then someone gave me this book.

The Spirit of the Lord told me that whenever I was about to get a sore throat, just stop eating right then, totally; and do not eat for three days. I did that; and the sore throat went away. I did not catch a cold. That was the only way I could ever come out of a sore throat without getting a cold. That happened several times. So I would continue these fastings. I would do about three every year. So, for years, I never got colds. That was the immediate benefit from fasting. It kept my weight down to normal. I had more energy because I did not have excess weight to carry around. It just worked in my life.

The first day of a fast, you are extremely hungry; and you think you are going to starve to death. On the second day of a fast, you just have to overcome this. You have to drink a lot of water. Water sometimes stops part of the hunger. You need to drink pure water. Your taste becomes real sensitive. You must like the taste of the water. The second day, you start to get somewhat weak from not eating.

Then the third day, my strength came back to me. I had no desire to eat. The hunger left. I actually felt like I was floating in the air. I could not even feel my feet on the ground. It was just a beautiful sensation that I had this first time I fasted for three days.

YOU CAN START FASTING

First, you have to make a decision that you are going to fast. Then you decide when you are going to do it. If you are a person with a lot of energy, you may not have to pick a special time. I worked a normal day, no matter what I was doing, when I fasted. After I had fasted several times, I did not have the problem with the sore throat; I would pick Monday, Tuesday, and Wednesday.

You make the decision first; then you just step right in and you do it.

The benefits of fasting are beautiful because of the many things that happen to you after you have fasted. Prayer is answered much faster in your life, in the spiritual realm. Scriptures seem to come more alive in the spiritual area. The physical area is so practical and easy to lose weight like that. You lose one full pound of weight a day whenever you fast and you do not eat anything.

At the end of three days, when you weigh yourself, you will probably weigh five or six pounds less than what you weighed when you started fasting. Part of that will come back. You permanently lose three pounds each time you fast for three days. That weight stays off of you.

Fasting is so beneficial to the health of your body that even if you've had a problem of gaining weight, you will more quickly lose weight ... you see, these fasts readjust your system and your body. After you do these fasts for a period of time, you don't even gain weight as easily as you did before you fasted. The benefits are very great and multiple.

Not only is fasting scriptural and God urges us to do so, scriptural fasting is very beneficial to our well being both in the physical and spiritual areas of our life.

Stay in Your Church

In 1970 because of the many spiritual things that had been happening in my life, I told the Lord that I was studying the Bible and seeking an answer for a period of three years as to whether I was in the right church that the Lord wanted me in.

Also, before the three years were up, I started to be involved in evangelism in Full Gospel Business Men's Fellowship International, an interdenominational group that had members from all Christian denominations. The leadership in this organization consisted of very strong Christians who told the members to stay in their own churches. In 1973, between Christmas and New Year's Day and at the end of the three years, the Lord spoke to me very clearly at my church.

He said, "I want you to stay in your church, for I have a work for you to do there."

I was happy to know my Lord was not only inviting me to be there, but that He had given me a job to do. It took quite a while to get a Bible study going, but I think that is one of the areas that my effort has helped.

Bishop D'Antonio gave a very interesting and very

moving testimony concerning his ministry in Aloncho Province in Honduras.

TESTIMONY OF BISHOP NICOLAS D'ANTONIO

In the early part of 1976, Bishop Nicolas D'Antonio, a Roman Catholic Bishop, was residing in Columbia, South Carolina for thirty days as a guest of a local pastor. The bishop waited to go back to Olancho, Honduras, where on June 25, 1975 there had been a massacre in his parish. Nine priests, nuns, and lay church workers were killed and thrown into a 150 foot deep well and covered up.

The bishop was still alive because he had been invited to go to the 1975 Charismatic Renewal Celebration at the Vatican. He spoke at the monthly meeting of the Columbia Chapter of Full Gospel Businessmen's Fellowship International. I went to Columbia to hear him. The following is his full message taken from our tape of the meeting.

I would like to point out a statement by the bishop concerning the issue of salvation in the Catholic Church. He stated that ninety-nine percent of Hondurans at that time were members of the Roman Catholic Church, but many of these members were not Christian.

HOW PERSONAL RENEWAL RELATES TO CHURCH RENEWAL

For reasons I still cannot comprehend, on December 31, 1963, it pleased Pope John Paul VI to appoint me to a prelate neruose (boss of nothing is what the translation means.) It is one grade or one step from becoming bishop. The apostolic nuncio, the pope's representative, who revealed this confidential information at the time, apologized that I would not be elected bishop until later on. He said that I should accept the honorable appointment out of a sense of obedience.

Prelate neurose or bishop, the whole thing came as a great shock to me. Nevertheless, I accepted. The apostolic nuncio breathed a sigh of relief. If I had said no, that would set the church back maybe three years (laughter), in order to find another guy (more laughter). I was to be installed officially in the department at Olancho, Honduras, which is like a big state in the United States. It became a Spanish republic on March 17—St. Patrick's Day. That had nothing to do with my installation (laughter). My mother and my aunt came from the United States for the solemn ceremonies. The Honduran government and hierarchy went all out to make the event a memorable one in a negative sense, and it was.

I began my new duties with great misgivings of my unworthiness and lack of suitable preparation. I plowed through all the canon law to discover what my new duties were. The more I studied, the more confused I became. To follow the rulebook, I needed more priests and experts in different fields of service to help me operate the Episcopal Courier, a fancy name for the central office of administration.

There were only eight North American Franciscan priests and six nuns to attend to the spiritual needs of 145,000 people spread throughout a 13,000 square mile area, which I negotiated on mule back. I dared not sacrifice anybody for office work. That left me by myself in the Episcopal Courier. From March until September in 1965, I administered the sacrament of Confirmation, all about the Spirit, but the Spirit was not there. It was mostly administered to large numbers of baptized infants, sometimes as many as 700. I had a sore arm from putting my hand on all those heads. This was my pastoral duty, and at the time, it satisfied me that I was doing something.

An invitation came from the Holy See to attend the second half of the Vatican II Council, in 1964 and 1965. I found myself in St. Peter's Basilica, in a totally new world. I was a country boy and this was a big city. The proceedings were only conducted in Latin, and I discovered that I had forgotten most of the language. Therefore I missed a great deal of the meaning of what was going on. I later learned that there were other bishops and prelates in the same predicament.

As the days went on, Latin began to come back to me and I began to understand. What helped immensely were the speedy translations compiled by the priests who were experts in the various languages to help the bishops. The observers, the non-Catholics, had instantaneous translations. We, the dumbbells, had nothing. The documents were too numerous to read, let alone study them all day was impossible. I found myself cramming and trying to digest as many ideas as possible.

How could I vote for or against a council paper unless I understood it? I marveled at how 2,500 bishops could dialog as they did, sometimes employing powerful language, and yet not losing their serenity. We had miters and crosiers to hit each other with but we did not use them. It was obvious to me that the Holy Spirit just had to be there to keep this new Pentecost moving along.

When I got back to my prelacy or my diocese, after the first session of Vatican II, I found trouble. It was just beginning. A group of my best laymen were jailed and accused of communism. In their fervor, these native gentlemen would leave the city each Sunday to preach the Word of God in the villages and to sing joyful hymns of praise.

Because of my authority and personal friendship with the military major, I was able to convince him that these men were in no way communist agitators. He freed them, but fined them $7.50. Why, I do not know. This was my first serious encounter with our military authority.

In 1965, I went back to the Vatican II Council and this time I was much more alert to what was happening around me. I returned to my prelacy determined to put into practice what the Holy Spirit wanted for the Catholic Church—a house cleaning and updating. This meant no more triumphalism. I had the answer. It placed an emphasis on ecumenism through prayer, dialogue, and involvement so that men and women could build up the body of Christ and the people of God. The liturgy of the sacraments in the vernacular language, the discoveries of Vatican II, and the powerful declaration of the bishops of Latin America described in the Medellin documents of Columbia, South America spread through the Catholic Church. It put the Catholic world into a crisis like never in its history. This crisis trickled down to my local church in Olancho.

I got rid of the Episcopal throne, like the kings had, you know, in the Cathedral, and I stepped down to become one among equals. This apparent act of humility did not really take full effect until much later, when I was baptized *in the Spirit. Praise the Lord.*

I invited my clergy to study the Vatican II documents together in order to set up a pastoral program. Right from the start, we ran into difficulty. We discovered, painfully, that we did not know how to dialogue. Each pastor was a king in his own right. The bishop was also a king. We were all separated. It took about one year for it to catch on. In time our clericalism, the priests, had all the answers. It began to melt away but boy did it hurt.

I had primary and secondary schools that were forced to shut down because the parents were not keeping up the monthly payments. The parents said, "The bishop is rich. Let him pay for it." I was left with an empty building and a lot of irate parents. I badly wanted a good Catholic college, managed by Christian men and women. An apparent answer to my prayers came when three Christian brothers of La Sai accepted to take over the school. They lasted exactly one month. Someone stole the enrollment fee and only sixty-four male students matriculated. The building could easily accommodate three hundred and fifty students. I begged the brother to save the situation by accepting girls, but they said this was against their holy rules. With a brief apology, they packed up and departed.

This turned out to be a blessing in disguise, again the work of the Holy Spirit. We began to use the building for spiritual retreats, especially for men, and this drew excellent results. The group studies and the frequent dialogue brought about another significant change. Our school building graduated into a human promotion center, with a priest and a layman as director and sub-director. For the first time we got into the social field.

Before it was Jesus and I. Now our team studied the social and cultural reality of the area. Priorities were agreed upon and numerous projects written up for funding by sympathetic foundations. We learned that it was not enough to administer the sacrament only. We had to assist the marginalized peasants to wake up to a new life through prayer, study, and organization. We had well instructed social professors of the doctrine of the Catholic Church taught our parishioners how new life [in Christ] worked.

This work began to require money, so with two Christian lay leaders I went to Europe, Canada, and the United States to present our projects to different foundations. We were well received and our projects were approved, and the machinery of human promotion started to move. We invited the peasants and also the rich to attend the course on how to build a better world, starting on the home front. The elite refused to make an appearance.

Some people visited our center only to look for slogans or other material and quote them out of context. Soon we were labeled as Communists and foreign agitators. Threats were made against our lives, especially yours truly. I earned two beautiful titles, The Mad Communist Bishop and the Hangman of Olancho.

From the many types of courses given, soon all kinds of projects were born—both small and large savings and consumer cooperatives that never existed. They included chicken farms, well digging, road making, domestic nurses, farm techniques, sewing circles, women's clubs, food for work, social workers, schools, celebrators of the Word, the Holy Bible, prayer groups, radio Bible programs, and a whole lot of other things. Things! But without the Holy Spirit they stayed things.   We divided the parish work into a hierarchy of three levels: the prophetic, the liturgical, and the social. Directors of the different teams were named and the machinery began to function.

All went well except for the liturgical team that really never got off the ground, because we lacked trained personnel. From 1969 onward, things began to click. Olancho was looked upon as one of the most progressive churches, which was both admired and hated. Priests and sisters, who read about our work, came to visit, and then stayed to help.

In 1968, six priests and two sisters served the church population of 150,000. By 1972, the numbers climbed to eighteen priests and twenty-one sisters. Honduras is 99% Catholic, but not Christian. There is a big difference. We were told that we had more laymen working in the church as a body than anywhere in the country. I attributed this increase in personnel to the fruits of my own Baptism in the Spirit in 1970 and also to the Life in the Spirit seminars now taking place in the prelacy.

Having acquired a critical conscience, the peasants organized themselves into what they called the National League of Farm Workers. Thus united they could now bravely assert their rights and have a say in government affairs and decisions. This was a startling change of events for the government, and especially for the displeased landowners and cattlemen, who were accustomed to do whatever they pleased with their domestic servants and farm hands.

In fact it was their firm opinion that the camposinos were incapable of learning. Inclined by major promiscuity, lies, filth, drunkenness, and theft. From this reason the *peasant received extremely low salaries, like 50 cents a day. He had to walk two hours to work and two hours from work. They were undernourished and some of them had eight to ten children. Our compensation program followed the laissez-faire method and it brought the campisano to his true sense of human dignity—a child of God and as an equal with his richer brother. The earth was created by God and intended for the benefit of all mankind, not only for the select few believed to be favored by destiny, heredity, or politics. One day after a series of courses, a poor farmer remarked that he felt like he had been reborn. It is like I have come out of the dark into the light.*

Honduras has experienced fairly good agrarian reform, but due to the created interests of our groups, it travels at a snail's pace. The peasants observed that there was plenty of uncultivated land around serving no social purpose, and in many cases it was not even legally owned or registered. Because of dire necessity, they began to pressure the Agrarian Reform Institute and the government to accelerate the reform. If ignored, they threatened to recuperate the property, not steal it but take it back. In justice it belonged to them as Honduran citizens. They complained that more importance was given to a cow than to a human being.

The director of the local office of the National Agrarian Institute in Olancho was an opportunist who attempted to please both the rich and the poor. On February 15, 1972, he gave the go ahead signal to a group of organized farmers to take over a piece of property called La Lancara. About forty adult men with their wives and children settled in the area and immediately began to prepare the soil for planting, in time for the rainy season. The Honduran flag and placards were set up, which read,

"We Need Land to Work On. We want Justice and Peace. We are Catholics. We don't want violence. We want to dialogue."

The owner in question of La Lancara complained to the police. Several [police] arrived with the hope of convincing them to leave. They agreed on the condition that the owner himself come and dialogue with them, but he failed to show up. Instead he prevailed upon the director of the ENA, the institute to petition soldiers from the capital, to get the invaders off the property. The troops, ninety-five strong men, were armed with automatic weapons.

On February 18 at 2pm in the afternoon, shots were heard. Six camposinos were brutally murdered while their wives and children scattered in panic to save their lives. They lost themselves in the wooded mountains. Four others were seriously injured and two were taken prisoner after a cruel beating. The captain gave an order to charge and fire, and then a sergeant received a bullet wound in the back. I confessed the dying soldier and saw the wound for myself, a gaping bleeding hole the size of the palm of my hand.

The doctors diagnosed it as being caused by a high-powered rifle bullet. Naturally to defend themselves the soldiers and the enemies of the camposinos said that the sergeant died from a machete wound when attacked by the invader.

My efforts to get help were fruitless. Telegraph and telephone lines were cut off for four days by the rich. The bodies were left unattended until late at night. That same day my deacon offered to remove the bodies and take them to their families in the parish vehicle,   assisted by the brother of one of the dead. My deacon, now a priest, wrote a six-page description of this horror story that the nation's principal paper published in full. I authenticated the article with my signature. The news of the massacre scandalized and angered every strata of society and leaped out to the world press. The media blurted out its protest and demanded that justice be met.

In my homily that next Sunday, I exhorted my infuriated people not to resort to vengeance. They were out to kill all of the landowners. I encouraged a cooling off period and a time for reflection. I called that awful day Good Friday Anticipated. It was during the Lenten season, and we honored the brave men who died as martyrs. I called them martyrs. I encouraged dialogue on all sides and blamed what happened not on the rich, the soldiers or the camposinos. I blamed the massacre on the social injustice of oppressing the poor that was rampant throughout Latin America and the world.

Calling the invaders martyrs angered and embarrassed the government and the military. The nationally organized landowner and cattlemen association lashed out and attacked me personally in the press and radio. [They called me] the promoter of the land invasions, and the cause of the present strife. When things began to settle down the government sent an investigating committee to Olancho. In order to dialogue with the camposino league, the organized landowners and cattlemen and myself.

I opened the session with the quote from Luke 4:16-19. The meeting in the town hall was a farce. The camposinos were not justly represented. The majority of those present were the landowners and cattlemen and their friends. Although the meeting settled nothing, it did cool off tempers. I explained that at no time had I ever organized or encouraged the camposinos to "invade" private property or to utilize violence of any kind. I was sneered at and not believed. In a sense, I couldn't altogether blame the rich, because at no time had I openly condemned the invasions.

Why I didn't do so was that I was informed by the leaders of the camposino and the office of the institute that the recuperations were done legally, according to law. The law was plain. If property wasn't serving a social function, and the owner could not prove his legal right to it, then the peasants could take it. Despite the conflicts, we continued with our short-range priorities to seek out and educate natural leaders in our parochial centers, always keeping in mind the long-range priority. That is the building up of basic Christian communities centered around the Eucharist and the written word.

While the local church grew and matured, the old man Adam began to show his teeth. Some of the leaders began to place too much emphasis on the social aspect, so that prayer and especially the Eucharist were not always given their proper place. To keep them from going too far to the right or the left, spiritual retreats were given. But all heads are not the same. My most influential leader could make no distinction between faith and politics, the sacred and the profane. He drew other leaders after him, inspired with a legitimate ambition to form a political party and some day, through free elections, win high places in government to better serve the oppressed poor.

I had to exhort these well-intentioned men not to instrumentalize the parish centers and pastoral movements to gain followers for partisan purposes. I encouraged them to do this on their own time and to employ their own facilities as free Christian citizens have a right to do. I clearly pointed out that the church hierarchy could in no way favor any one political party, even though guided by Christian principles. As the bishop I am the father and servant of all men, not some men.

In order to rid the Olanchon church of the image it got for promoting a particular political party, I encouraged the leaders to work independently of the church. After much prayer and reflection and the approbation of my clergy and sisters, I symbolically sold them the human promotion center so that they could better manage their own affairs as organized workers and be free to join the party of their choice.

My priests and I would continue to assist them in their spiritual need and defend them in times of persecution. Our enemies were of course greatly dismayed by this turn of events and planned how to get the center for a school.

Allow me to describe to you may own Baptism in the Spirit. I'll never forget it. When our Blessed Mother became Spirit Filled after giving her consent she became the first liberated woman. I too, in a much lesser sense of course, experienced a liberation. Praise the Lord. Allow me to backtrack a bit.

During my seminary days, my study of Scripture was extremely theoretical, for which of course I blame only myself. Strong emphasis was placed on dogma and morals. Not that this was wrong, but something was lacking, although I could not place my finger on it. Once I was assigned to the missions of British Columbia, Canada, I soon tired of this same Scriptural reading Sunday after Sunday. This I also could detect in the faces of my parishioners who heard the gospels expounded on each year in the same way, and totally out of context with the experiences of their daily lives. So I went in for the telling of moral stories, which I found much easier, but with rarely a reference to the written Word. Gradually I got into the mental health positive thinking by Bernicats. I tried them all.

Not that these were bad either, but somehow things got man centered instead of Christ centered. And so far as the Holy Spirit was concerned, I mentioned him only when I blessed myself as Catholics do, Father, Son, and Holy Spirit, here he is or recited the official prayers.

In 1945, a holy obedience placed me into an entirely new world—The Spanish Republic of Honduras, Central America. I did there exactly what I did in Canada, with an emphasis on doctrine and the sacraments. Evangelism, as we understand it today, didn't even occur to me. All the people were Catholics. My job was done once I got a sinner to go to confession and to receive Holy Communion at least once a year—big stuff. From there on salvation was almost automatic, so they could sin all year, go to confession once, and be set.

Confession and communion increased appreciably, but I witnessed few true conversions. Something was lacking. Many who occasionally received the sacrament returned to their old way of life, such as drunkenness, concubinism, adultery, theft, and vengeful murder, while they were going to church. The social life remained the same, with bad politics, illiteracy, lack of hygiene, lack of doctors, health centers, roads, and the media.

There literally existed no social conscience. It was my family or just me. The usual explanation offered by the people was that God so willed it. I am poor because I am poor. He is rich because he is rich. God willed it. What to do to destroy this false resignation. Pope John XXIII, God bless him, got the answer when the Holy Spirit inspired him to celebrate an ecumenical council which the cardinals gave me a demonstration. On the spot, they gave me a demonstration that convinced me that I was right. This happened in 1944, pretty far back, at that time when I didn't fully realize that the Holy Spirit worked outside the Catholic Church and with everybody, even women.

You see during my seminary training we were taught that the Pentecostal experiences were reserved only for the first Christians to help get the preliminary church firmly on its feet. Well, in 1969, I began reading non-Catholic literature about Pentecostalism. I learned that Methodist ministers were being expelled from their churches because they had become Pentecostals. Presbyterians, Anglicans, Lutherans, and Baptists were thrown out too.

I wondered that this was strange. Here we have ministers who love Jesus, who love people very much, and yet they are labeled agitators, and even heretics, no matter (big boss is talking). They have set the peace in order of the institutional church. They set division. They must be expelled, complained their superiors. Cardinals, bishops, priests, sisters, and staunch Catholic gentlemen aired the very same complaints, whenever a member of the flock witnessed his Spiritual Baptism. But isn't it true that Jesus Christ is the greatest divider of all ages and paradoxically the greatest unifier. You can't beat the Lord.

Nonetheless, I concluded that these educated ministers had something that I didn't have—a new way of life. They risked their official ministry and all the money implied rather than betray what the Lord Jesus gave to them. I wanted the same and badly, and even looked about me for a Catholic Pentecostal to ask for the laying on of hands. At that time I could find no one. Naturally I was well aware of the fact that I was baptized sacramentally with water and the Holy Spirit, confirmed, ordained into the Catholic priesthood, and now as a consecrated bishop. How much spirit did I want? Definitely the Holy Spirit resided in me, but it was much like water in a tightly capped bottle.

I felt compelled to answer this question. Am I truly allowing the Holy Spirit in me to do his thing, his way? (Galatians 2:20) One day while alone praying in my chapel, I experienced the Baptism in the Spirit. I began to cry uncontrollably. I shed tears, joyful tears, every night for weeks. I was very content and full of sweetness, yet there was something that bugged me—the question of tongues. "Lord, I pleaded, give me everything, but tongues."

It took me one whole year to discover that tongues was the easiest of the gifts. I ended up singing in tongues in spite of my bad voice. I began to tell anyone that would listen about my new experience. I went back to reading the Scriptures with extraordinary interest, as I hadn't done before. Of the numerous spiritual books I read in my life, the Bible was not one of them.

Perhaps I should say how the Holy Word literally sprang to life for me. It sprang to life due to the power of the Spirit. The daily recitation of the hours that all Catholics have to say each day became no longer a chore.

There was no rushing to finish the breviary and the mass to get them over with. Another discovery was the power of praise. Oh yes, I praised the Lord many times but somehow doing it now was different. Most of my life, I was accustomed to the prayer of petition, but today praising God became happily liberating and something I could do frequently—everyday. The exhortation of Christ to pray always now made perfect sense to me.

My first experience with prayer groups was terribly embarrassing. The raising of arms, clapping, rhythmic body movements, in time with the music, and spontaneous prayers all struck me as disorderly, even irreverent. I had to literally perspire before I was able to break through my inhibitions. It was like taking off my pants in public. That's a fact.

What a relief it was to be able to pray with other people on an equal basis and to allow the Holy Spirit to work his way mysteriously into the minds and hearts of the assembled worshippers—what a difference. In the beginning when I attempted to interest my clergy and laymen in renewal, I received sympathetic smiles. But for some reason I did not get through to them. I got the same cold shoulder from six out of seven bishops in Honduras.

One bishop said, "Nick, Come on, cut it out. I'm a bishop. You're a bishop, right. We're consecrated, right, and who did the consecrating? The Holy Spirit. Yes, that's right, and there is an old lady telling me that I have no faith. She is a Pentecostal, telling me, a bishop, the defender of the faith, that I have no faith. You're all crazy."

They said, "Look Nick, prove it to me." I'm not a charismatic in the sense that you are thinking about. Prove *it to me that the miracles in the first ages are happening today. Prove it. Would you take a glass of poison milk right now in my presence? I said, "Bishop, for heaven's sake, the Scriptures don't read like that. I am not supposed to poison myself to prove a point. The trick is that if I am given a glass of poison milk and I don't know about it. I drink it and don't die. Well that's the proof. But I'm not going to tempt God to prove it to you."*

Another bishop said he would never change. "I am Catholic, and you are doing what Protestants do." I talked to another bishop who was starting to change. He said hey Nick, Give him one year and he will change too, but he kept on running. "I will never change. You are a bunch of kooks. He said let's give him two years.

In 1970, I wrote to Ralph Martin. God bless Ralph Martin, he did so much good. I wrote to ask his community to pray for renewal in Olancho. I couldn't convince anybody. I assumed that my letter strayed because I never received an answer. But in 1975, five years later, one of those surprises of the Holy Spirit [happened]. Ralph Martin found my letter and informed me that due to prayers, the renewal in the Spirit caught on in Honduras and prayer groups were popping up everywhere. I was surprised to hear that.

To prove this, he sent me a list of addresses and another surprise. He invited me to be a bishop patron. Even better, he invited me to attend the 1975 International Conference on the Charismatic Renewal in the Catholic Church. I didn't like that at all. I wasn't interested in going to Rome. But after much pondering, I accepted. In some mysterious way, the trip to the Holy City saved my life.

Had I returned from Rome to the prelacy as I had planned, I would have been the tenth body, along with two priests, two women, and five laymen, discovered in a deep well located in Losporconas, Olancho. Now with respect to the repeated threats on my life, Archbishop Elder Camera, also called the red bishop, expressed my sentiment well, concerning the consequences to the church.

Like Christ, he boldly sided with the oppressed poor. He evidently wrote for the government and the privileged that didn't want to loose their absurd and abusive privileges. The church was judged as unfaithful to its religious mission and a subversive agitator. There are suspensions, persecutions, incarcerations, torture, and death, at least among priests and religious [leaders] and among all the laity, also martyrdom for a bishop. It is a humiliation to remain free like me. I should be dead, whereas in his place, laymen, religious [leaders] and priests suffer. Quotation from Elder Camera.

A group of powerful landowners and cattlemen convinced the present military government that the Olanchon church and the organized peasant farmers planned to overthrow the regime with machetes on June 25, 1975. The peasants organized a seven-day hunger march, not only in my prelacy, but throughout the nation to protest the snail pace of the agrarian reform. At 2am the same day, the government troops raided at gunpoint and ransacked the bishop's residence, my house, the rectory, the convent, the centers of human promotion.

They also arrested the personnel, during their attempt to take over my center of human promotion called Santa Clara. On February 18 to commemorate the martyrs who died on that date. Four campisanos and one soldier were killed, and the building, a donation by the church to organize campasinos, was confiscated. A little past midnight, two of my priests, two visiting females, and five laymen, who worked in the promotion center, were questioned brutally and shot to death. Their bodies were dumped into a 150-foot artesian well that was dynamited and covered with grass to hide all clues.

I was informed of this tragedy on June 26, the next day, while I was on a preaching assignment in Baltimore, Maryland. I was exhorted by my clergy, and later by the apostolic nuncio, the pope's representative, not to return to Honduras because a price was offered for my head. The blow was a hard one, and I leaned on the kitchen wall to keep from falling. In a flash, I vividly recalled a scene during the last general meeting I celebrated with my clergy, sisters, and lay leaders a few months before the massacre of June 25.

Fifty-three persons were present in all. Threats against us were now getting stronger. I asked them if we were still willing to continue to function as a prophetic church—to announce the good news and to denounce the bad news—I explained the possible consequences, persecution, crime, expulsion or even death. Nobody protested.

But one camposino leader stood up and said, "I'm scared, but if Christ were here that's the kind of church he would want. And I praise the Lord for it. In very truth, had it not been for my Baptism in the Spirit; the kind words of consolation by Pope John Paul VI; the solidarity of organized groups throughout the world; and the wonderful example of the people who participated in the 1975 International Conference on the Charismatic Renewal of *the Catholic Church, I would not have been able to bear this latest cross. Although at this writing I am still outside my diocese. I don't despair of going back. And from the bottom of my heart, I even went to prison the other day to visit the men that killed my men. I embraced them. I forgave my enemies and I earnestly pray that someday they may become my brothers. I praise the Lord for the greatly comforting act of my clergy.*

It was a miracle. Sisters were back in their mission working quietly and with great valor—a miracle in itself. Rumor had it that soon even before the crackdown all foreign priests would be expelled permanently. Not only from my diocese, but from other parts of the nation as well. My greater joy however is that the church of Olancho can boast of its modern martyrs to inspire and to intercede for us before Christ, in the constant building up of the kingdom.

Several events culminated in the massacre of June 25, 1975. In April of 1971, the association of cattlemen and farmers of Olancho accused the bishop and the human promotion center for promoting land invasions. This was in the headlines in the national paper. The pastoral team denied the accusation in the same paper. Agrow and the camposinos were invited to a radio forum to clarify the church's position. Agrow members were indignant and did not appear. Youth groups and camposinos supported the bishop and his collaborators. Men and women of a nearby marketplace barred the cathedral doors while the bishop investigated the incident the angry crowd chanted: We want Honduran priest. We don't love you bishop. Get out.

Two years later, these same protestors apologized to the bishop and explained that they were forced to insult him or lose their places in the market. And I blessed all of them with gifts.

Agrow (the rich people) placed their tractors in front of the bishop's residence and declared a strike for one year, killing all of their calves. No cows were milked for one year. It didn't last that long. Threats against the bishop's life began to reach him and his friends begged him to escape. Late that night in the parish of Casta Camera, a group of men painted the walls of the city with letters SRED. No one to this day knows what those letters meant. They set off dynamite in front of the residence of Father Evon Betincore, now a martyr. He refused to be intimidated and made every effort to dialogue with his enemies.

In September of 1971, the bishop was greatly consoled by letters of solidarity on the part of the apostolic nuncio, the Honduran bishops, and their native clergy. In October of 1971 a bomb scare against Father Betincore continued although the priest was in no way guilty of the attack. The president of the country believed the enemies and wanted to expel the priest. The bishop convinced the president otherwise.

In April of 1972, a drunken police chief struck down a catechist in the bishop's own home and then arrested the bishop, a lay brother, and a catechist. The bishop was questioned and scolded for two and a half hours first and then released to please Father Dadella who happened to know the police chief and convinced him of his error. The arrest embarrassed the government. The chief of police was removed to prevent a revolt on the part of the camposinos.

In May of 1972, there was an investigation of the Antoncara murder. The president sent a colonel, two congressmen, and a representative of the National Agrarian Institute, the president of the national association of camposinos of Honduras and a military observer to interrogate the bishop's possible affiliation with communism. The results were favorable toward the bishop. This was incredible, but it was never published so as not to embarrass the government and the rich farm owners.

In December of 1972, there was a military coup. We have a new government every two years and one president is out and a new general is in office. This does not affect our pastoral work. In the summer of 1973, land recuperation spread throughout the country and was supported by a temporary decree. Landowners complained bitterly to the press and threatened to pay mercenaries to eliminate camposinos and church leaders. In April of 1975 the Wall Street Journal reported that United Brands bribed high government officials with $1,250,000 so that they would not raise the banana export tax, which was called the Bananagate Scandal.

In April of 1975, the investigating committee was organized and the general's strong man was overthrown in a bloodless coup. A new president took over and ruled with a council of twenty-seven men. In May of 1975, again there were mass invasions by the hungry camposinos. Armed forces gave them forty-eight hours to disband. They obeyed after a quiet dialogue, but succeeded in extending the land reform process. In May of 1975, the bishop left for Rome to attend the Third International Conference on Charismatic Renewal in the Catholic Church. His double purpose was to express his fidelity to the Catholic magisterium and to promote the renewal in the church.

In June of 1975, the bishop cancelled his trip to return to Olancho and rescheduled it for June 27 to please his mother. His mother was alarmed when the Eastern Airline flight crashed killing one hundred and ten passengers on June 14.

On June 25, the day of the massacre, a departmental supervisor of primary schools organized a group of schoolteachers and children, assisted by members of the Agrow, to enter the human promotion center to take over the building. Shots were heard. Soldiers streamed into the edifice and four peasant leaders and one soldier died on the spot. Thirty-two people were arrested. When the hunger march was on its way to Tegucigalpa, a seven-day walk from Olancho, it was stopped by soldiers and disbanded without incident.

On June 26, the government troops raided at gunpoint and ransacked the bishop's residence, the convent, the parish centers, and at the same time Jesuit centers in Tegucigalpa. The capital of Honduras suffered the same fate. A group of Canadian priests, several Olanchon priests, sisters, and two seminarians were captured and flown to the capital as prisoners.

Father Evon Betincore was in Tegucigalpa to pick up his mother and sister-in-law and sent them by plane to Hoolagalpa, where my cathedral was, to save his mother the wear and tear of a five-hour car trip. During the drive, Father Evon and two girl passengers were kidnapped in Losporconas. His mother never got to see him again. After torture by emasculation and a forced confession on tape by Father Evon, Father Michael Sizner and five camposino leaders were murdered and their bodies were thrown into a 150-foot artesian well. The American press was strangely silent and the Columbian embassy pressured the Honduran government to investigate the disappearance of Father Evon and the two Columbian women. The Catholic Church of Honduras demanded an explanation for the massacre and asked the president to free the detained priests, sisters, and composinos.

In June of 1975, the bishop was told, by phone, not to return to Honduras until further instructions came from the Holy See. A $10,000 price hung over his head. A Honduran bishop took his place until things calmed down. In July of 1975, because of the strong protest of the Honduran university students and other complaining groups, the government was compelled to dig the bodies out of the well with tractors. After almost five days and nights of excavating, nine bodies were recovered and fingers were blown off and in horrible condition.

On July 19, 1975, with this news the bishop entered Honduras by way of Guatemala, and he was unsure of arriving there. Upon his arrival, the apostolic nuncio said in shock, "Nick, you should be in the States." But bishops, clergy, and sisters were happy to have their bishop back. It was the work of the Holy Spirit that brought me back. Had I received the letter from the Holy See, I would not be in Honduras that day.

The military investigation of the high command gave a detailed report of the crime and arrest of those culpable. The day before the Columbian government pulled out its ambassador and protested for the death of Evon Betincore and his future sister-in-law, Maria Balgas, also a Columbian.

In October of 1975, for the first time the three organized camposino groups formed a national united front, representing 30,000 families. They gave the government an ultimatum of twenty-five days to hasten the agrarian reform. The director of the National Institute of Agrarian Reform, a lieutenant, backed up the camposino drive and was soon expelled and accused of communist tactics.

In December of 1975, the president and two of his counselors elevated their ranks to brigadier generals. There was no word. At this time hope for dreams that 1976 would be a better year died hard for Honduran camposinos.

The small businessmen succeeded in getting the military government to dialogue with almost every branch of organized society. This was a definite step forward. The object was to set up a representative council to aid the men in power on how best to serve the nation. New voting statutes were to be drawn up and an election time was set. These were a terrible surprise.

The traditional parties and the elite wanted the election much sooner, but the camposinos preferred to go along with the military. They knew that the nationalists and the liberals were great on promises but slow on executing their promises. They had the ambition to organize a popular labor party or give their support to a totally new form of government.

It was summer again, now 1976, and the camposinos published this statement: Unless we can possess our own piece of property, we shall continue to recruit men again and again even if we must die doing so. Their heroes were the martyrs. The Catholic church and other churches were good examples of cooperating with the camposinos.

I want to conclude this narrative on my personal renewal and its influence on the local church with a statement by the archbishop. The Archbishop Elder Camera of Olinda offered a timely warning for the local church. "We must avoid that the oppressed of today *become the oppressors of tomorrow." My personal renewal influenced my own thought about the church. The economic and social development must not be obtained at the sacrifice of religious life. While working with the poor, we shouldn't hate the rich. Not for a moment should we forget that the soul of evangelism is the Holy Spirit. We are only the instruments, and we shall not be utilized unless we are humble and full of hope, joy, and love. Jesus Christ is Lord. God bless all of you.*

That statement by Archbishop Elder Camera of Olinda struck me as a very wise statement. It is a truism to the extent of the future. We have to be very careful. People get very calloused very quickly. If we are a poor person, and we get a job and start making money. We build a nice house and buy an automobile. We jump up to the middle class of our area. If we are not careful, we are very quick to think we are better than they are. So we all have to guard ourselves against that type of thing. I have seen it happen many, many times. Even children put their parents down.

Christianity makes a difference in a person's life. Our spirit becomes born again. The Holy Spirit puts compassion in our heart to replace callousness. He will fill us with love. Even then we have to be careful to guard our lives. We can never step on someone else to climb the ladder of success, even after salvation.

So many people have been members of churches in Central America. But all they needed was a personal relationship with Jesus Christ. That is the great hope we have today, to bring Jesus Christ to the masses. Jesus will help every situation and problem that we see today in the nations of the world.

10

Vatican II Council Importance

In August of 1960 the Commission of Faith and Order of the World Council of Churches met in St. Andrews, Scotland. David du Plessis was asked to be one of the speakers. Three hundred of the top church leaders in the world were there. Brother David was asked to speak on the Pentecostal experience. He was told to be frank because he was among friends. The people attending knew there was a difference between themselves and Brother David.

Pope John XXIII sent Father Bernard Leeming, a theologian from Oxford University in England, as his representative. Brother David said that he did something that he rarely ever did. Because his time was limited he typed his speech so he could limit it to fifteen minutes. This would allow for forty-five minutes for questions and answers.

After the meeting Father Bernard Leeming went up to David and said, he had never heard that Christ was the Baptizer of the Holy Spirit. He asked to get together with him to discuss this. It was fairly late in the evening so Brother David said what about breakfast the next day. They agreed to do that.

When they met in the morning, David asked Father

Leeming how he slept. Father Leeming replied that he didn't sleep very well because he kept thinking about what he heard about Christ the baptizer of the Holy Spirit. He had gotten out his concordance to look for this. He couldn't find it right away so he looked under a different heading and found it in Matthew, Mark, Luke, John, and Acts. Finding the issue three places throughout the Bible proved how conclusive Scripture can be.

Father Leeming asked Brother David to give him the blessing of the Baptism of the Holy Spirit. Brother David told him that he could not give it to him. It did not come through apostolic succession. He said that he must ask Jesus for it in prayer, and then he would receive it. Then Father Leeming asked how he knew when he had it. The answer he received was that tongues are the least of the gifts of the Holy Spirit. It is the first one that you receive. At the time of speaking in an unknown language, tongues, you will know that you have the Baptism of the Holy Spirit or the Pentecostal Blessing.

It is my understanding that when Father Bernard Leeming reported back to Pope John XXIII at the Vatican he took with him this Pentecostal blessing, with the gift of speaking in tongues. He gave his full report to his boss.

I believe that this is probably the first person in modern times, in the hierarchy of the Roman Catholic Church, who came into the Pentecostal experience, by speaking in unknown tongues. I have not been able to find any member of the hierarchy of the Roman Catholic Church for the past several hundred years or so, who has spoken in tongues through the Baptism of the Holy Spirit, up until this happening.

August of 1976, I was strongly urged by the Holy Spirit to go to the Montreat, North Carolina Bible Conference. David du Plessis was one of the speakers at this conference. Brother David was an observer throughout all of the Second Vatican Council. He met many cardinals and bishops and when it was over he had some friends among them.

One day while talking to some of these friends this is what was told to him, as to why and how Pope John XXIII came to the decision to convene the Second Vatican Council. One evening when it was getting dark, the Pope was sitting in his residence at the Vatican and a bright light lit the room up and the voice of the Lord spoke to him. He said, "I want you to convene a Vatican Council." The following evening the same thing happened a second time. He called some of his advisors together and told them what had happened.

As he was telling them, he broke down and wept. Some of them commented that he was getting old and senile. He told them that was what he wanted to do, and he asked for them to do a preliminary study on whether or not they could do it. When the study was finished they came back and said that the cost would be so tremendous that they could not see how it could be done. Pope John said, and I quote, "The Lord wants it. He will pay for it, and we will do it."

I had been searching for an answer to a question for about eight years. My question was, did the Holy Spirit really lead the church Fathers during the Second Vatican Council? On Thursday night Brother David spoke to the whole 3,000 who were gathered in the large auditorium and he spoke for over two hours. In the middle of his speech he got off of the subject he was on, answered the question that was on my mind, and got back on the subject.

Brother David said that a bishop came up to him one day and said, "Brother David, do you think we are being led by the Holy Spirit?" "Bishop," Brother David replied, "Aren't you moving and breathing and getting things accomplished? How else could it be done? How else could you have done what you are doing unless the Holy Spirit was with you and leading you?"

On Friday and Saturday it was a great privilege to sit for another three two-hour session with Brother David as he commented on God's Word as the Holy Spirit gave him the areas to talk about. I felt like I was in the presence of the apostle Peter himself.

The great thing that I see with the Second Vatican Council is that in every area, I believe, that they went into, it brought the church closer back to the Bible. It brought the Church back to a greater understanding of the scriptures, the importance of the scriptures, and closer to the scriptures in every area that they went into during that Second Vatican Council.

Many changes came about. They were all in that direction. It came out of a historic time into a greater light that the Holy Spirit had brought forth to the Church.

In 1978 and 1980 I attended both of the World Conventions of FGBMFI in Anaheim, California. Those were the years that I came to know Fred Ladenius, the former Vatican Press Secretary for both Pope Paul and Pope John Paul. Fred sat on the platform and was in the business meetings during those conventions.

At the time Ralph Wilkerson was pastor of Melodyland Pentecostal church, which was right across the street from the main gate at Disneyland. The day after one of those conventions Fred was the speaker at the Melodyland Church. He spoke on his testimony that day. He is a very interesting person. Sara and I went there to hear Fred speak. Here is a bit of his testimony as to some of the things that has happened in his life:

"It was in Rome in the early seventies that I first met Demos. I knew already that Pope Paul VI had been desirous to thank Demos personally for the spiritual renewal which had spread out to the Church of Rome. This renewal which had been so greatly influenced by Demos' vision.

David Duplessis, who was highly esteemed by the Pope, had been the first to bring him news of the wonders that the Holy Spirit was operating across the ocean, and upon hearing David's words Pope Paul VI had uncharacteristically exclaimed that this was an amazing gift that God was bestowing upon the church.

At the time I was a foreign correspondent for various newspapers and televisions and as a member of the Vatican Press Corps, I was in daily contact with the highest political and religious authorities. Just a few years earlier a friend and colleague at the Vatican, Father Gaudet, a Canadian priest, one Saturday afternoon had invited me to come with him to an English-speaking Catholic charismatic prayer meeting at the Rome Jesuit University. For the first time in my life I saw people, mostly nuns and priests actually, lifting their hands and praising God in strange languages. That same evening Father Gaudet took me to a Pentecostal Church, which had been built by an American pastor, John McTernan. Again, I saw people praising God in this same and totally new way. I was baptized in the Holy Spirit that very night and soon after started the first Italian-speaking Catholic Charismatic prayer group in Italy. Soon I was being invited by Catholic Churches all over the country to speak of this incredible renewal: the Holy Spirit's outpouring all over the world. It was an amazing time.

John McTernan, who by that time had become a dear friend, told me of the FGBMFI airlift to Rome. He told me that I should meet the founder of the Fellowship, an American Armenian businessman who had received a powerful vision from God, Demos Shakarian. The Vatican is a unique observatory where you can meet the most extraordinary people. I had met John Kennedy, Adenauer, Charles de Gaulle, Lyndon Johnson and so many more. Anyone who was anyone would sooner or later come to those ancient halls. Upon meeting Demos I was struck both by his simplicity and his wisdom, and by his complete dedication to the vision he had received so many years before. This dedication which has proved to be so contagious, inspiring hundreds of thousands of men to join the Fellowship and reach out to the outermost corners of the earth. Right away Demos invited me to speak at the meeting the Fellowship had organized at the Rome Conference Centre that weekend. It was the beginning of my involvement in the Fellowship and the start of a friendship with a kind and courageous man.

The following summer it was my privilege to be a main speaker at the World Convention in Anaheim. I was soon asked to move to Brussels as the editor of the various European editions of Voice magazine at the new European HQ. I traveled all over the world to speak in chapters and conventions: Africa, Australia, Latin America, behind the iron curtain and in every European nation. I would often repeat or emphasize what Demos had said so many times, in accordance with the Apostle Paul, "It is not our mandate to build new churches on foundations laid by others. Our vision is trans-denominational!"

I now live in Lugano, in the Italian speaking part of Switzerland. My ministry is mostly focused on Italy through television and radio and evangelization and teaching, meeting throughout the country. I am Director at large of the FGBMFI, President of the Lugano Chapter, and very much involved with the Fellowship in Italy. We now have chapters in Milan, Venice, Rome, Turin, Bari, Verona and Mantova.

Presently, our dynamic and inspired International President, Richard Shakarian, leads the Fellowship into the third millennium. He has not veered off course from his father's original vision, but has given it a renewed energy and relevance for these times. And it is only the beginning..."

Breakthrough Businessmen

The Spirit of the Lord had prepared me for the Full Gospel Business Men's Fellowship International (FGBMFI). I was actually looking for an organization like that. The Lord was dealing with me personally. I was looking for an organization that was heavy on winning people to the Lord. I was ready for it!

When all the guys shared their short testimonies at my first breakfast, they all told about how they got saved. They were talking; this was the very first time (12-14 guys) I had ever heard that God talked to other men. I was just so happy and so elated; all I could do was sit there and weep (for joy). I did that every week for about three months. There were others like me.

Demos Shakarian, a dairy farmer from Downey, California, tried to start the first chapter of the Fellowship, but nothing happened. After one year of weekly meetings he decided to give up, but he was going to pray and seek the Lord one more night. That December night in 1952, God gave him this vision.

"I could see the people on the earth—millions and millions of them standing shoulder to shoulder. My vision seemed to move in. I could see tiny details of thousands and thousands of faces. And what I saw terrified me. The faces were set, lifeless, miserable. There was no real contact between them. They stared straight ahead, unblinking, unseeing. With a shudder of horror, I realized that they were dead . . . ."

"The vision changed. Whether the world was turning, or whether I was traveling around it, I don't know. But now beneath me was the continent of South America. Then on to Africa, Europe, and Asia. Once more the startling close-ups occurred, and everywhere it was the same. White faces, brown faces—everyone rigid, wretched, each locked in his own private death."

"Lord!" I cried. " What's the matter with them? Lord help them!"

"My son, what you see next is going to happen very soon."

"The earth was turning—or I was moving around it—a second time." Below me again were millions upon millions of men. But what a difference! This time heads were raised. Eyes shone with joy. Hands were lifted towards heaven. These men who had been so isolated, each in his prison of self, were linked in a community of love and adoration.

Asia, Africa, America—everywhere—death had turned to life and the vision was over. I felt myself returning to earth."

This vision is told in the book *The Happiest People on Earth.* Demos tried, but could not start one chapter.

-120-

When he turned it over to the Lord, chapters sprang up everywhere.

When Demos died in 1993, Richard Shakarian, his son, became the International President of the Fellowship.

I distinctly remember the 1989 World Convention of FGBMFI was in Rio de Janeiro, Brazil. I felt like I should go to this convention so my wife Sara and I decided to go. We drove to Miami and flew from the airport there. In the airport while boarding the plane, we met John and Louella Schmook, who were from Oklahoma. We spent some time together there, and over the years have become very good friends. While we were in Brazil, we also met Henry and Myra Swindler, who were from Los Angeles, California. Henry, being a Swindler, was Chapter Treasurer of the Santa Ana Luncheon Chapter of the Fellowship. Since the World Headquarters of the Fellowship was in the Los Angeles area, and we also became friends of the Swindlers on the trip, we usually stopped by to see them on our Fellowship business trips to California.

One day Myra was talking about Gary Greenwald, her pastor. She said, "Let me tell you how I met him even before he was a preacher and pastor of a church." One day the Lord spoke to Myra and told her to go tell this sign painter that the Lord has called him to be a pastor. She said, but Lord I don't know him and I don't know where he works.

Then the Lord said, "I will show you. When you come to this next street turn left, go four blocks," and when she got that far the Lord said, "Now turn right. Go two more blocks, and now turn left. Go one more block and as soon as you cross the next street pull over and stop." She looked up and was in front of a sign painter's shop. She went in the shop and asked for Gary. She told him that the Lord had sent her to tell him that he had been called by the Lord to be a pastor. He said at the time that he never thought that he would be doing anything like that. But it wasn't too long before he found himself in Bible school, studying to be a pastor. And he did become a Pentecostal pastor. When we were there with them, several times we attended the Eagles Nest Pentecostal Church, and he was the pastor. At least on one occasion Pastor Gary was one of the youth pastors whom we had for the young people's program at our World Convention in California.

Myra and Henry were elderly, and they went out for a lot of their meals. One morning they were driving past the Headquarters building in Costa Mesa, and the Lord spoke to Myra and told her to tell Demos, the International President of FGBMFI, to sell the building. Henry looked up at her about that time and saw an odd look on her face. So he said, "Myra, what's the matter?" Myra told Henry what had just happened, and then she said, "I don't know when I will ever see Demos again."

About two weeks later Myra and Henry were at the Santa Ana Luncheon Chapter meeting. They had a good meeting and were in the car ready to leave when Demos pulled up, got out quickly, and went into the meeting. Richard, Demos' son, was with him. He went by the car, and Myra told Richard what the Lord had told her to tell Demos.

She asked Richard if he would tell Demos for her. Richard said, "Myra you know dad and you should tell him yourself." So in the meantime Demos was talking to the men who were still in the meeting room. He said the Lord said someone here has a word for me. Myra spoke to Demos and told him, "The Lord said it was his will that the headquarters building in Costa Mesa be sold." Demos told all the men there that the Lord had to send a lady to give me this message. Shorter after this Demos died. His death was in July of 1993, a few days after the Boston World Convention.

I have attended all of the World and National conventions since 1976. The Directors' Annual Meeting is always held during the World Convention. While Sara and I were at the Rio de Janeiro, Brazil World Convention in 1989, Demos' assistant called me on the phone. He said Demos was appointing me as an International Director of the Fellowship. He would like me to take my place at the International Directors' Meeting today. The South Carolina Chapters voted me in at a later date.

The book, *The Happiest People on Earth,* tells the story of how FGBMFI began. In 1952, God gave Demos a vision of the Fellowship, and it was started from that vision. Before Demos died, he appointed his oldest son Richard to succeed him as the International President of Full Gospel Business Men's Fellowship International. Richard was confirmed by a directors' meeting at a later date. We did sell the headquarters building after Demos' death. The Lord has seemed to direct all of our important decisions in the Fellowship as we have sought him in prayer.

The Fellowship is presently active in approximately one hundred and sixty countries. Its membership is open to all Christian denominations. Each year for the past few years it has been responsible for over one million personal commitments to the Lord Jesus Christ. During 2000, this figure was dramatically increased. The Fellowship is the largest network of Christian businessmen, who are laymen doing evangelistic work, in the world.

In May of 1998, Richard Shakarian, International President of FGBMFI, and his wife Vangie attended the Italian National Convention of the Fellowship in Venice, Italy. Mr. Shakarian wanted to stop in Rome on his way back to America, but he was having some difficulty finding a hotel room there. Some of the Italian leaders heard about Mr. Shakarian's plight and so they told him they thought they could help him.

One of the top Catholic charismatic leaders, His Excellency Archbishop Luigi Accogli, Archbishop of Rome and Apostolic Nuncio, was at the Italian Full Gospel Convention. The Italian leaders introduced Richard to the Archbishop. The Archbishop told Richard that he would take care of it for him.

When Richard and Vangie got to Rome they found out that they had a whole apartment right next door to the Archbishop's residence. The Archbishop showed them around the city of Rome. He arranged for an audience with Pope John Paul II. One day the Archbishop showed Richard a parcel of land with a building on it in a prominent spot between the airport and the gate to the city. He told Richard that FGBMFI ought to buy the property. He said he would like to see a monument placed there for the bringing together all of the Charismatics and Pentecostals of all of the Christian denominations, as a common place and a monument to the Holy Spirit.

Richard invited the Archbishop to be his personal guest at the 1998 World Convention of the Full Gospel

Business Men's Fellowship International in July in Dallas, Texas, U.S.A. That evening the Archbishop declined the invitation. The next morning Richard had a phone call. The Archbishop said that during the night the Holy Spirit spoke to him. He said, "These men are full of the Holy Spirit and he ought to go." The Archbishop came with his secretary, who was an Irish nun named Sister Martha. Although the Archbishop speaks and reads a number of languages, his English was not fluent. Of course Sister Martha spoke fluent English.

The convention lasted five days, Tuesday through Saturday from 8:00 a.m. to about 11:00 p.m. He attended most all of the sessions and during the evening sessions he sat on the platform. He was introduced to the audience on several occasions, and he was the major speaker on Thursday evening. He spoke in Spanish, and we had live translations. I met the Archbishop and talked with him a good bit, and we traded business cards. He said he was very pleased with the evangelistic work that is being done by the FGBMFI.

However, a big surprise to me was that one year later at our 1999 World Convention in Anaheim, California, his Excellency Luigi Accogli returned to that convention. He brought a gift to our International President Richard Shakarian from the Pope and some kind words of appreciation for the work of the Fellowship. He again was a speaker at that convention. One day while there, he came to one of our Directors' business meetings, with a word from the Lord that the Holy Spirit had given him during the night for the Fellowship. In August of 2000 the Archbishop came to his third world convention in Miami, Florida.

THE FUTURE: YOUNG BUSINESSMEN

In 1996 two young businessmen received salvation and were turned on for the Lord. It was an exciting day in San Pedro Sula, Honduras. Dennis Aplicano (21 years of age) had just left his life of gambling and drugs and was now completely dedicated to Christ. The business he owned as a young businessman began to turn around, and his faith caused his business to increase.

Dennis Aplicano and Kiki Morales, his close friend, began to work together. These two young men remembered the prophecy that had been given to them at the 1997 World Convention of Full Gospel Business Men's Fellowship International in Houston, Texas. Even before they had fully committed their lives to Christ, the prophet had told them that they would lead a vast army of on-fire young men and women, bringing the nation to Christ. They began to form FGBMFI youth chapters. All over their nation revival swept the universities. Postgraduates began joining the youth chapters. That was the beginning of a great spiritual renewal of the youth.

Many hundreds of young people joined these chapters in Honduras. Kiki asked Richard (International President) to come to Honduras for a rally in the fall of 1998. He went from meeting to meeting for two days, and thousands of youth came to these meetings. The young people called FGBMFI the Fraternity, and it became a very popular meeting place for them in Honduras.

HURRICANE MITCH

The last day of this Rally, Hurricane Mitch was moving into Central America. Over ten thousand people were killed and missing. There was massive destruction to four countries in Central America—Honduras, Nicaragua, El Salvador, and Guatemala. Eight thousand of the known dead were in Honduras alone. At least 70 percent of the economic infrastructure in Honduras and Nicaragua had been totally destroyed. Flooding and mudslides wiped out roads, bridges, telephone lines, and almost every other means of communication. Banana and coffee crops—the dominant exports of the region—were virtually eliminated.

Richard Shakarian said, "What can we do? I feel like we must do something." So a planning meeting was called for January 15, 1999 in Miami, Florida. About one hundred leaders came from almost every country in Central and South America and the U.S.A. I was asked to come to this planning meeting. Bill Brunson and I drove from Charleston, South Carolina.

Friday night Richard poured out his heart. After showing videos of revival among the young people in Honduras to the leaders in Miami, the fire of God exploded in their hearts. Prophecies were given and plans and ideas came forth. God seemed to be targeting Nicaragua.

Nicaragua, one of the poorest of all the Central American nations, is a country where there is sixty percent unemployment. Hunger, illiteracy, and bondage abound there. As we spent time in prayer, we believed that God could break that bondage and send great revival. The Lord started putting plans in some of the men's minds. Saturday we looked at the plans and it seemed as though we needed to have an evangelistic outreach to that devastated part of Central America. But what country and when? We could only do so much at one time.

Richard presented what the Lord had spoken to his heart. We should have a special outreach to the country of Nicaragua. There was immediate fire in the hearts of the men who heard the plan. By the next day the Lord was starting to provide ideas on how we could impact that entire nation during an outreach of about one week. Also the Lord had spoken to Richard. We need to move to a new level in the Spirit. Because there is such urgency we feel and believe our time is short. We believe God has mandated the Fellowship to start touching entire nations all at one time.

Richard said the moving of the Spirit reminded him of what had happened in Honduras. He had a special outreach and touched approximately 2,000 young people – not knowing that the plane he left the country on was the last commercial flight out of the nation before Hurricane Mitch hit. Within the next couple of days the entire airport was flooded with 20 feet of water. Many people lost their lives. Could this have been the last opportunity for some people to receive the Lord?

Many times over the last couple of years, the Lord has spoken to different men and women of God from all over the world, and said that the Fellowship would be used mightily to help bring in the last-day harvest of souls. It is interesting to know that even that week some of the intercessors in different parts of the world mentioned they felt America is hanging in the balance. We must pray and reach out like never before. If our legislative leaders do not do what is proper, God will judge this nation. We have tried to be sensitive to the Spirit of the Lord. When we hear His voice, we try to do everything in our power to fulfill what He has told us to do. But, also we need the help of others. I pray the Lord will let you feel the cry of our hearts to impact the nations, because the primary focus of this

Fellowship has always been to win souls.

We, as an organization, are not limited to just reaching souls. We have programs that feed and clothe the poor. We also have programs that visit prisons, hospitals, and retirement homes.

At the same time the Lord was speaking to Richard Shakarian, a vision was given to one of our chapter presidents in Nicaragua. He saw a vast field of ripened grain with the number 20 upon it. A voice said, "In four months will be the beginning of the harvest of 20 centuries." We reckoned that this would be the first week in May 1999, so the timing was set by the Lord. The FGBMFI led the way to reach at least one person for the Lord in every one of the one million families in Nicaragua. We called a worldwide fast for one day a week until May 8. Monday May 3, 1999 would be the first day of our outreach.

The first day in Nicaragua, I spent several hours in a planning session at their national headquarters of Full Gospel. Much prayer had gone up as part of the planning. Wednesday through Saturday were the big days of the outreach when hundreds of men and women went out to planned meetings, but at these meetings many more meetings were taking place. Many people were being healed, delivered, and ministered to as God's army went out.

MY MEETING WITH DANIEL ORTEGA

A group of us went to the home of Daniel Ortega, the leader of the Sandinista Party, for a meeting. He had been president of the nation for eleven years.   There were seven of his men in the room and fifteen of our people. When Daniel came in, he sat down between Richard Shakarian and Dr. Humberto Arguella, the president of FGBMFI for Nicaragua, who had gone to school with Daniel Ortega. Richard spoke first, and then Ortega spoke. Richard told him what we were doing and why we were in Nicaragua. He said that we did not pick the date to visit his country. God picked the time. He said it was a time of crisis, and this crisis might be greater than any of us thought. At this point, Richard said the anointing came on him and he was speaking prophetically. He said, "Daniel, God is saying that you are a great leader and that you care for your people. You have a love for the poor people. If you pray for your country, God will answer those prayers. We did not come to supply your needs, but God will supply those needs for you."

At this point Richard asked Daniel if he could pray for him and he acknowledged that he could, so Richard held his hand and prayed. When he stopped praying, he asked Daniel if he wanted to pray for his country. It was quiet for perhaps half of a minute, and then Daniel prayed a beautiful prayer. After this the meeting was over. We all stood up, took pictures, gave farewell greetings, and left. It was about 7:30 on Thursday evening.

On Saturday, after the final Rally, we were back at the hotel in the early evening. Ortega's group called Richard and asked him to come over to a celebration they were having. The first meeting was a bit tense, but this one was very casual. One of their men was talking about hearing Daniel pray. He was so tickled by it that he laughed so hard he almost fell off his chair. They were shocked because they had never heard him pray. Now a number of his people belong to the Full Gospel. And that night, Ortega asked Richard if he would come back on July 19 and speak at the annual Congress of the Sandinista Party to about one thousand people.

The Lord opened all the doors to Full Gospel in Nicaragua. There were five of us in my fire team. One day, we went to the women's prison out in the country where there were ninety-four inmates. We were there for almost two hours and held a prayer service for them. About sixty-five of them were in the prayer service. We sang gospel songs. Two of us gave our testimony. DeCarol Williamson preached and gave the altar call. All of them came up for the altar call to give their hearts to Jesus, and we led them in the sinner's prayer.

When God opened the doors in Nicaragua, the anointing of the Spirit of God came down. People's hearts were open, and there was a mighty move of God. We had five hundred and twenty-five scheduled meetings, but as we went to these meetings, the people had other meetings for us to attend. The meetings grew to about nine hundred by the end of the week. We did not have time to attend all of the meetings, so the local Full Gospel members finished them. We had members there from at least seven different countries.

At the Saturday evening rally, Dr. Humberto Arguella had added up all of the people who were ministered to and who were touched by the Lord and led in the sinner's prayer. Up until that time, the number totaled approximately ninety-seven thousand people.

REPORT: TAKING A NATION FOR THE LORD

By all reports, this dynamic event even surpassed

anything the FGBMFI has ever done. With over 925 meetings taking place, the impact could be felt to the very fiber of the nation. The momentum was so powerful that meetings have continued even since the outreach had ended, even into the years 2000 and 2001. Unprecedented numbers of people were healed and committed their lives to Jesus Christ.

From the national newspapers to television, the outreach was a major topic of the news, bringing a positive message of hope to a country which has had more than its share of challenges of late. One headline read, "A World Leader Comes to Nicaragua." The people were wide open to receive FGBMFI International President, Richard Shakarian, representing the 160 nations in which the Fellowship is active.

There had been several prophetic words concerning this event in Nicaragua, indicating that we should go there and when. Richard Shakarian had to delay his planned departure by two days due to the civil strife, which had closed the airport. The timing of the FGBMFI outreach turned out to be ideal. A week earlier would have been impossible, but by the time the teams arrived, the people were looking for a miracle.

The FGBMFI was graciously received by Sr. Arnoldo Aleman, President of Nicaragua, as well as by the opposition leader, Daniel Ortega. They prayed with these key men, and for the nation as a whole.

The youth teams went to schools, colleges, and universities to share their testimonies and the good news about Jesus with students. They were received with enthusiasm and openness. This group alone counted 24,353 young people, who invited Jesus Christ into their lives during their meetings.

At the police academy, we spoke to the future law enforcement officers of the nation. A high percentage came forward for prayer to commit their lives to Jesus Christ.

Factories closed down their operations while FGBMFI men came in and spoke to their workers. Central American members were taught to give their simple testimonies, telling what God has done for them in terms that people will understand. They prayed for both management and employees.

Now other nations want us to come to them and do the same thing—not holding religious meetings behind closed doors, but going out to where the people are, praying for them and sharing the simple truth of Jesus Christ. Richard Shakarian prayed for the nation on the most popular secular TV interview show. There were so many invitations for teams to speak that it was impossible to get to all of them.

Jamie Sol, from El Salvador, reports that it was like being at a train station. There was so much happening that it was like catching a train. Every few minutes one was going someplace new—it was only a matter of getting on board! The group that came from his nation went back on fire with excitement about what God can do. They had seen the blind see and the lame walk, but more importantly, they had seen how God could use them to reach people for Jesus.

When asked what they thought about it all, the group from Panama could only say, "It's incredible! We have never seen anything like it. It is more than we expected."

This was the vision of the FGBMFI in action. It was a mobilization of ordinary people, each one armed with a single confidence, "God can do it." Whatever the need, "God can do it!" God opened the way even in the area of the geological situation. The active volcano, which had been causing difficulties of late, did not stop the teams. At the schools people came to the teams confused, "What is happening here? That boy who is weeping on the floor is the worst in the school." Jesus had touched him and he was on the floor praying.

From the north to the south, from the east to the west, a work has begun that will now spread throughout the whole world. God showed FGBMFI President Richard Shakarian the time and places and confirmed it through many others. As it turned out the outreach took place at a strategic time for Nicaragua something no man could have anticipated. It was the time and place for miracles.

FGBMFI provides a vehicle that ordinary people can work with and work through and be much more effective. It is not my way. Our God is a supernatural God. On the Day of Pentecost He sent His Holy Spirit down to earth to the 120 in the upper room who were told to wait for Him. Jesus told them not to go out and try to minister until they received the Baptism in the Holy Spirit. If we are obedient and listen to the ways of our supernatural Lord, many things will change. Anyone can be effective to win the lost to the Lord, to pray and the sick will be healed, and to mend the broken-hearted. The Great Commission in the Gospels has called us all to do this work of evangelism.

The Holy Spirit is really preparing the way and leading the way. Anyone can be effective to win many people to the Lord. The Great Commission in the Gospels has called us all to do this word of evangelism.

If a person was looking for spiritual things, there could be a lot of reasons why someone would join the FGBMFI. The first thing, you would hear testimonies of a person who probably had some problems. You could see that those problems were solved, in the person's testimony.

Testimonies are stories of people, and they are probably one of the most interesting things that you could listen to, because there is always something in there that affects you or something that has an answer to something you have wondered. It is so enlightening and so changing, the people are so friendly and so loving, that it draws persons like a magnet, because as they lift up Jesus in these meetings, Jesus draws all people to them, and to people that are ministering for Him. That is what happens in FGBMFI.

FIRE TEAMS IN HONDURAS

After the outreach in Nicaragua, other countries wanted the same in their country. It was decided to go to Honduras one year later, in May of 2000. The outreach was from May 15 through May 20, and my wife Sara went with me on this trip. The first part of the week, I ministered in the hospitals. The nurses were on strike, so many family members stayed with patients in the hospitals. This gave us the opportunity to pray for many more family members. All day long, we would go from room to room praying for their healing and for jobs, businesses, and incomes. We led them in a prayer of salvation as the Holy Spirit would lead.

In this hospital our interpreter's name was Victor. He was a 62-year-old dentist who lost everything in Hurricane Mitch. He lost his house and his office. And to save his life, he tied himself and his wife to a tree with a chain. He does not have an income now because he lost his office and all of his dental instruments.

Another place I ministered was a high school, where there were larger numbers of people. We usually gave one or two 10 to 20 minute testimonies of how Jesus came into our lives, then we had an altar call and led the ones who wanted to accept Jesus in a sinners' prayer. At this particular high school there were a number of fire teams working. It was a large school, and when we were ready to leave we had a list of approximately 45 students who wanted to start a FGBMFI chapter in the school. Some of these students had heard about the youth chapters that had been started by Dennis Aplicano and Kiki Morales.

A number of people were struck by the openness to accept the Lord all over the nation of Honduras and throughout Central America. Wherever we asked people to come to Christ, they willingly and gladly gave their hearts to God. I have never seen such hunger for God before in my life. I believe one of the major things that happened in Central America is that we learned how to mobilize this tremendous army of FGBMFI to touch entire cities and nations throughout the world.

At the university, a young lady gave a folded note to one of our fire team leaders. She said, "I don't need this anymore." It was a suicide note. It read, "Dear Pappa, Dear Mama, I love you very much, but I have no hope. That's why today is my last day." She had told her friend she would kill herself that day, but instead, our Fire Team gave her a message of hope. She received the Lord and no longer needed the note.

The doctors' offices were jammed with people because the nations' hospitals were on strike. At one point a doctor came out of his examination room and asked a nurse, "Where are all the patients? This room was jammed with patients only an hour ago." She said, "I am sorry, doctor, but the men from the Full Gospel Business Men came and prayed for the patients. They all left."

Congress invited Richard Shakarian to speak. After his message they gave a standing ovation. Many declared their faith in Christ. The Defense Minister and Chief of Staff called a special meeting of all the High Command. About 150 men stood with Richard as they prayed the sinners' prayer. Then they went on to the military academy, and the Air Force. From there they went to the 105th Brigade. Throughout the television news and talk shows, there were many commitments to Christ.

We went to people in factories, stores, universities, prisons, hospitals, military bases, businesses, marketplaces, and government departments. Meetings were conducted where businessmen, forgiven by Christ, gave their stories. The effect was electric as scores of individuals in each place received the Lord.

International Executive Vice-President John Carrette said, "In Honduras I saw the fulfillment of what few have understood." In the book, *The Happiest People on Earth*, FGBMFI founder, Demos Shakarian, says, "When Dr. Price first began to prophesy these things during World War II, it seemed impossible that untrained people could have the same impact as the great evangelist, like Charles

Price, himself. What an irresistible force it could be if hundreds, thousands of such men were to band together to spread this kind of good news all over the world!"

No evangelistic effort has had the impact in Honduras that FGBMFI men did in May 2000. This could be true of every nation!

I think this is the greatest miracle—untrained people having the same impact as a great evangelist! It goes to the very heart of the Vision. As we keep inspiring the FGBMFI leaders to send out their men, they will see what Demos envisioned: ordinary men have the same impact as great preachers!

International Director Ron Weinbender made the observation that:

We just experienced the greatest outpouring of the Spirit of God in the history of the Fellowship! It is the beginning of what the Lord is doing through this mighty organization called the FGBMFI. The mandate we received from the Lord is to "take the nations."

We are touching top leaders. In Honduras, the Lord opened the door to every high level of government office in the nation, including the judicial system, the military, the Congress, the Mayor's offices, Police Departments, and the Chamber of Commerce. We are so grateful for the individual sacrifices made by everyone who participated in this nation-impacting outreach.

My question to you is, "Where else could you literally impact every level of society?" God said by His Spirit that "this Fellowship will be used mightily in the last days to bring in the Harvest" and that "the latter days will be greater than the former days even though we have been around almost 50 years." We are just beginning to fulfill the vision that God gave Demos many years ago.

Col. Daniel Lopez Carballo, Chief of Armed Forces for Honduras, is the top ranking military leader. He is one of the hundreds of thousands who accepted Jesus Christ as Lord and received salvation during our one-week outreach in Honduras. There was a great change in his life because of this. He was having problems in his marriage and it was coming apart because of the dark side of his life.

In August of 2000 the World Convention of FGBMFI was held in Miami, Florida. Col. Lopez was one of our speakers.

I want to share his message because it is typical and it shows the change that only the power of God can bring to an individual. When individuals are changed then the nation is changed. And as in Honduras when hundreds of thousands are changed by the power of God through salvation, the impact is so great, it changes the very fiber of the nation. As like Bishop Nicolas De Antonio said, so many men come to church occasionally, but they are not Christians. They are church members only, and do not have salvation.

Col. Lopez, Chief of Armed Forces, gave the following message at the FGBMFI World Convention in August 2000. It is excerpted from Voice Magazine:

Ethical, moral, and spiritual values are of paramount importance to our nation today. I have served in the military for more than 32 years. Over my career I have received many honors and decorations. It is now my job to work closely with the president and the government. In spite of the prestige of my position, I know there is something more important than earthly success.

There is awareness in most of us today that we are empty. Though not everyone is willing to acknowledge it, the fact is that we need Jesus Christ. With this in mind, when I exercise my authority, I want to keep integrity as number one in importance. In the Armed Forces we have officers, non-commissioned officers, soldiers, marines, technicians, professionals, and working staff—all under my authority. This is an awesome responsibility, and yet the most important thing in my life is the deep change that God has made inside me. I understand so clearly now that I am nothing more than a simple mortal.

Every man, whether high or low, will finish his life like every other man. It won't matter if he was rich or poor. God has opened my eyes to see that all we have is so very temporary. We are only passengers in this life. He has caused me to rethink my attitude towards material things. He has shown me a new way, with His help, to serve God, my nation, the Armed Forces, and my people. His Holy Spirit gives me the wisdom, strength, and patience to serve well.

Institutions undergo transitions, and we have just undergone such a change. This one gives us opportunity to act in the best interest of our nation. God has given me a new vision for the times in which we live. We have just begun a new millennium, and because of this, our minds are focused on the future and a positive transformation for our nation.

There are people under my responsibility who also need to change, and we are working on this. I am introducing fundamental policies within the Armed Forces from the inside out. We have opened the doors to human rights organizations, as well as to the press, who have come in to witness the changes. We are walking in openness. With God's help, we will develop what our nation needs—a new Armed Forces working for the people like never before.

The Armed Forces in this nation is an organization that has promoted development. When Hurricane Mitch struck our nation, we mustered our resources to serve the people. We are there to fight narcotics trafficking. We want to help all our people. However, I am convinced that we will never achieve our goals without implementing a high moral and ethical standard, with the help of God.

Attitudes must change. We have told our officers that we must provide leadership, working together for the good of our nation. We must work together in harmony, and also with prudence. My country and our whole world need Jesus.

I have witnessed extraordinary things. I know the power of God works. It has made an incredible difference in my personal life. I have an inner strength now and I can sense the presence of God with me everywhere I go. He has reconciled my own family, and has given me ideas that only He can give. Some of the officers around me can not understand what is happening. I now have a freedom and act without selfish motives.

I tell them that if we receive the freedom and peace Jesus Christ gives, we will have a different approach to our positions in the Armed Forces. We will be dignified. Recently I was in a meeting with the commanders of the military. At the end of the meeting, I told those leaders that we must have faith, and we must be faithful. God has given us so much, yet often we fail to thank Him for all His blessings.

I no longer need to seek position. Now the most important title I hold is Daniel Lopez, son of God. I am the servant of my people and not the big chief. It is my mission to teach men and women to walk uprightly in honesty and transparency. In this way we will bring changes to the world around us.

I have promised God in front of the president that I have changed. I tell the military leaders that we need to allow God to change us and that, with His help, we will become better officers and will be able to effect positive changes in our nation.

There is one thing I would like to pass on to military leaders around the world: Our profession should be one of honor and sacrifice. It is also one of discipline. It is important that we lead with values. We cannot allow our standards to deteriorate. It is important to see God's hand in our decisions. We must be examples to our societies with God at the head of our lives. We must be good fathers. If God is with our families and us we can do our jobs with loyalty and honor.

Our subordinates look to us for leadership. We must be officers of God. I am the Chief of Staff in my country, but more importantly, I am a servant of God, my family, and my people.

Compare the difference to this leader's statements, and the way that he leads the men under his control to what happened in Honduras in 1976, during the time Bishop D'Antonio was there.

See the difference that saved and born again Christians can make in a nation compared to church members who are not Christian or saved as Bishop Nicholas D'Antonio stated the situation while there. In 1968 the Holy Spirit spoke to me in an audible voice and said there are many people in your church who are church members only and do not have salvation.

Dr. Pinel, the FGBMFI President of Honduras, reported that based on written reports submitted to his office after each meeting, he calculated that 326,800 people made a commitment to the Lord Jesus Christ during the Fire Team outreach in Honduras. This number does not take into account those who responded to testimonies broadcast over radio and television every day.

Dr. Pinel said when Richard Shakarian told us about the vision to reach one person in every family we were overwhelmed by the magnitude of this task. Nevertheless, in the belief that it was from God, we went to work in prayer and planning. In so doing, God gave us a plan to have at least 3,000 meetings throughout the nation. By the time the five-day outreach was over, this number had grown to almost 3,500 meetings in businesses, factories, government offices, and universities.

On Saturday evening we had a victory celebration. In my city a procession of 100 cars drove around the city seven times, blowing their horns, waving our red flags of faith, and shouting proclamations of victory. After the sixth time around, a beautiful rainbow appeared in a complete circle around the sun. We knew that God was pleased with our work in Honduras.

We are confident that there are very few people in our nation who did not hear about the outreach and our testimonies in one way or another. Richard said shortly after a planning trip, and a few days before the outreach started, he prayed, "Lord, you told me to reach one million people, one person in every family in the nation. They are open, but the 3,500 meetings being put together for our Fire Teams are not enough to reach a million people. You would not have told me to reach someone in every family if it were not possible. Lord, what are we supposed to do?"

It was then that the Lord took me back to Joshua when they were about to destroy the big walls of Jericho. These walls represented sin, iniquity and bondage. There was one lady in that city, Rahab, the harlot, who said, "I've heard of your God and we know that He is powerful in heaven and He is powerful on earth. I want my family to be saved." She was told, "Take a red cloth and when our soldiers are coming into the city, put the red cloth in front of your home, hang it out the window and everyone in your home will be saved."

The Lord instructed me, "Go to Honduras early. Take this message to the television stations; declare to the people throughout the land that they should give a signal of faith to God, and a signal to our Fire Team soldiers that they want their family to be saved and their business to be blessed."

I landed back in Tegucigalpa several days later. Immediately, the Holy Spirit took charge of my entire agenda. Within one day, I found myself on national television, one of the most powerful secular stations. For twelve days in a row, twice a day, on news shows and on talk shows, I gave the message of hope, "You have suffered greatly, and God has heard your cries. You've had Hurricane Mitch, deflation, business failures, bank failures, hospital closings, crime, floods, and famine. God has heard your cries, and He has come to deliver you. He sends us to give you the message of hope that from this day on, God is going to bless this nation. We are here with over one thousand Fire Team Members in 3,500 meetings, in every part of Honduras."

"It may be difficult for you to get through to us on the phone, or to contact us in person, or for us to find your place. So if you are not already scheduled for one of those meetings, and you would like your family to be saved, then take the same signal that this lady in the Bible did. Take any piece of red cloth and put it in front of your door, in your window, in front of your house, in front of your business. It will be a signal to God, for God's blessing, and as our Fire Teams are going down the street, when they see your signal, they will come and pray for you."

The last time it was done in a nation was over 3,000 years ago when the great deliverer, Moses, told the nation of Israel (which was in slavery at that time in Egypt) that God was going to bring them out of slavery, poverty, and bondage. Take the blood of the lamb, which stands for the blood of Jesus Christ, and put it on your doorpost, put it up above your door. Take this red cloth and put it up there. It is a signal to God of your faith, and if you do this God will bring you out of bondage. A few days later they were brought out of bondage with silver and gold, and not a feeble one among them. Slaves are poor, but God forced their enemies to give them silver and gold. Slaves do not have good health, but He fed them and He gave them their strength and health."

"Today most of your hospitals are closed down because of strikes, but I want you to know that the Healer is not on strike. Today I saw on the news that many of the small banks have been closed and many of you have lost all your money, but He that provides the silver and gold to this world is still in business. And He has got the power to bring deliverance to you today. Put up your red flag of faith and our Fire Teams will come and pray for your business, your home, [and your salvation]."

In Nicaragua during the one week in 1999, 97,000 received the Lord. With the local chapters continuing the work that had grown to over 250,000 one year later. In the year 2000 we also had outreaches in El Salvador and the city of Brownsville, Texas, which touched many people. On October 20, 2000 the government of Honduras invited a number of us to come back for a celebration. They were so happy with the work of the fellowship and the impact that it had on the nation that they bestowed on our International President the highest honor they have, which is usually given to presidents of nations. It was a beautiful celebration and banquet in the Princess Hotel in their capital city of Tegucigalpa.

When I was in the Hotel Victor, our interpreter, came and greeted me. He said, "George, remember the young man we prayed for in the hospital with kidney failure? The Lord healed him and I see him back on the street!"

A MAN CALLED GEORGE

12

Climbing the Ladder of Success

The Word of God says, "Thus faith comes from what is heard, and what is heard comes through the word of Christ." (Romans 10:17)   The more that you hear the scriptures, the stronger your faith becomes. The more you are able to walk and be with the Lord, to trust Him and believe Him, as you do those things, you will receive the blessings of the Lord. The greatest blessing is to know that you have salvation of the Lord. The salvation of the Lord is the greatest miracle. Healings are great miracles. The wisdom and the knowledge and the understanding that the Lord gives you for your everyday life, especially in your business, and your income, and everything that you do, should be a walk, tied in with your walk with the Lord. By reading the scriptures, you strengthen every area of your life. You get closer to the Lord. You have more peace and more joy. You learn not to worry about things. That is the greatest way that you can become an overcomer.

GIVING WILL CAUSE SUCCESS

In the early seventies an evangelist came to preach at the Charleston Holiday Inn, on the corner of Meeting and Calhoun Streets. For three nights at the end of his services, he prayed for the sick and invited people to pray the

-147-

sinner's prayer for salvation. At this time I was learning about giving and tithing to the Lord in the Bible. I usually put a dollar in the offering on Sunday at church—which was about it. The Bible has much to say about tithing or giving ten percent of your income to the Lord.

Malachi 3:8-10 says that if you do not give ten percent to God you are robbing him, and you are cursed with a curse. But if you do bring in the ten percent and put it in the offering he will pour you out a blessing that there shall not be room enough to receive. I quote Malachi 3:8-10 "Dare a man rob God? Yet you are robbing me! And we say how do we rob you? In tithes and offerings! You are indeed accursed, for you, the whole nation, rob me. Bring the whole tithe into the storehouse, that there may be food in my house, and try me in this, says the Lord of hosts: shall I not open for you the floodgates of heaven, to pour down blessing upon you without measure?"

Luke 6:38 says "Give and it shall be given to you; good measure, pressed down, shaken together, running over, shall they pour into your lap. For with what measure you measure, it shall be measured to you." At this meeting the evangelist said that he needed ten people to give one hundred dollars so he could continue to do the work that the lord had given him to do. He also said that those who gave one hundred dollars would receive a thousand fold from God.

An odd thing happened to me at that meeting. I wanted to give that man a hundred dollars and I didn't care what he did with it. I told my wife and we decided to give the money. I only had eighty-eight dollars, so I gave all that I had. Within a few months a man came up to me and offered me exactly $100,000.00 more for a certain property than I had invested in the property. I was sure that the Holy Spirit was teaching me about tithing and giving.

By giving, God blessed me even more. That is very scriptural. The Bible tells us to tithe, to give one-tenth of our income to the work of the Lord; and that we would be blessed. Giving is like planting a seed. When you plant that seed, you pray about it for the purpose that you ask God to take that seed and multiply it. You plant it and use it, so He can multiply it. He said He is going to return it to you.

It will be returned to you in the same measure that you mete it out; as you give it, it will be returned to you. In a practical aspect of it, in my business, I use that particular idea of giving. I was in a real estate investment business for about 40 years. I had apartments in the area where I lived. I would take the average rent in my area and I would deduct say $15 less; and I would rent my apartments for say $15 below the average price that other people were paying in my area. Then I was giving a gift, I was planting a seed, I was giving a gift to my business people that rented apartments from me.

I found out over the years, not only was it a great help to my business. God blessed me because of this gift that I made to these people. It was returned to me. At the end of the year, these residents stayed a longer period of time. In my business, the greatest costs would be, a lot of people change apartments every year, but my people would stay at least 2-3, 5-10 years. I had about 15% of my people would stay 5-20 years in an apartment.

It saved me a lot of money because I did not have to repaint these apartments every year. These people were happier. They paid less rent. It was a real blessing to me. As a practical thing, I shared that with other businessmen.

There are several different ways that tithing helps us. The Lord commands us to do it, for His works. You will get blessed from it also. The first time that I started to learn about tithing, I went to an evangelistic meeting. The minister who was preaching said, "The Lord told me to buy a tent and go to Arizona and preach to the Indians. I need ten people in this group to give $100 so I can do what the Lord told me to do." All of a sudden, the Holy Spirit was working with me, when I heard him say that...he said that God is going to bless these people and return them $100,000!

I really didn't pay attention to that. I got this odd feeling, because I wanted to give this evangelist $100. I was not used to doing that. I would put my $1 in the offering every Sunday when I went to church. And that was about it. This feeling kept persisting in me. So I said to my wife, "Sara, what do you think we ought to do here?" I first talked to myself, "Duggan, something is the matter with you. You want to give him 100 bucks out of your pocket?" I thought about it again. But the feeling was still there. I said to my wife, "Sarah, I want to give him $100. What do you think about it?" She said, "Well, if that is the way you feel, I guess it is all right." So I checked my wallet. It was towards the end of the month. I only had $88 in my pocket. I had never tithed before. I had never given that much money. I went ahead and gave it. I gave $88.

A year or two before that, I had bought this old building. I never thought it would be worth more than what I had invested in it, about $100,000. After I gave this, a few weeks later, a man came up to me on the street, and offered $200,000 for that building. That was $100,000 more than I had in it, and what I thought it was worth at that time. So the Lord really convinced me at that time that tithing worked. I knew the Holy Spirit was in that.

Since that time, we've made that decision and we have tithed to the Lord; and it works. We've gotten out of debt. A few years after that, by 1985, we had paid all of our debts and were on a cash basis, other than mortgage loans on buildings. After that time, the Lord blessed us financially. We got out of debt.

The "secret of success" is to have a good plan for your life, to have a good work ethic for your life; and be able to work hard at what you do. Follow the plan. I even had an alternate plan, if one business or one thing did not work out. As you have your life's plan, then work the plan. Do not give up. If it is a little hard to start with, just keep going. Don't forget to pray about what you are doing; and seek the wisdom of the Lord in it.

There are several ways to measure success. The success of the world is not necessarily being successful in the spiritual realm. To be a truly happy person, I do not think one can have true happiness and true contentment in one's heart, without being a fulfilled Christian. Without knowing personally the Lord and Savior Jesus Christ, because He is the One who created us, can fix up, leads us and guides us, gives us wisdom. We can study a book, but to use it with wisdom and use that knowledge, we cannot use it to the full advantage unless we know the Lord Jesus Christ.

He gives us that extra thing that really makes us

successful in every area of our lives. A success that is lasting, not here today and gone tomorrow, as we see so many people. But if you are walking with the Lord, you know Him and trust Him, and believe Him, you have that background. Then you will be successful. He will aid you to be successful in any legal business venture that you go into.

If you are successful in the business world and in your home and family life, that will attract some attention. That, in itself, will be a strong witness to some people. They will want to be like you. They come to you and ask, "How did you get to do this?" First things first. You know the Lord Jesus Christ. That is real success. That is the whole story in its entirety.

Conclusion

A Passion for Souls

The most important thing you can possess in your spirit is to have a personal zeal to win others to Jesus Christ. That happened to me after my salvation. That desire grew as I grew in the Lord. It even grew more after I studied the scriptures, and received the Baptism in the Holy Spirit.

The Baptism in the Holy Spirit was a great change in my life. I was a very shy person, especially in school and college. In law school, I had a very difficult time even reading from a book in front of a class. I couldn't speak in front of people at all. After I was baptized in the Holy Spirit, it was the first time I was ever able to speak in front of a group of people.

In FGBMFI, testimonies are a big thing. I was at a convention and I saw a lady who was very shy and scared, but she had such a powerful testimony that she wanted to give it, and she wanted to tell the story, and she asked this gentleman who knew her very well to come up with her and just stand by her as she spoke and told a little of her testimony. When I saw that, it really strengthened me. If this lady can do that, after that, I was asked to give my testimony, and I gave it for the first time at one of those conventions.

I was able to speak in front of a group of people for

the first time and tell my story about what happened in my life, my testimony about Jesus and how I received Him into my life.

It is extremely important to share what God gives to you...with your children. The way we did that, of course we always prayed with the children when they went to bed at night. We gave them Bibles when they got big enough to read. We spent a lot of time with them. We took them to meetings that we went to, including Bible studies. We always went to church.

As they became of age, we took them to evangelistic meetings. We took our four children to an evangelistic meeting one time, when an evangelist came to Charleston, our oldest child was 14-15; the youngest was about 6-7. To our surprise, this evangelist gave an altar call; and all four of them got up without our coaching or saying anything, they walked down to the front and they prayed the prayer of salvation with all four children.

We took them for the purpose of wanting them to come into a personal relationship with Jesus Christ. We wanted them to go to heaven whenever they died. We wanted them to have a personal walk with the Lord. We did not have a drug or drinking problem with our children.

In the years when our children were growing up, I attended a prayer breakfast every Saturday morning. The children took turns going to the breakfast, and I would take one each time.

With two of the children, they both received the Baptism in the Holy Spirit at the breakfast when they were about twelve years old. Our youngest son received when he was nine years old in 1977 at a youth meeting during the FGBMFI World Convention.

It was a great spiritual help in their lives. Because of this they attended church regularly right through their college years.

In 1973 I received the baptism of the Holy Spirit at one of the FGBMFI Chapter meetings. I was nominated for Vice-President of the local chapter of FGBMFI. I could not be an officer unless I had this blessing. Those were the rules of the Fellowship and FGBMFI followed the Bible very carefully because they did evangelistic work.

I sat in a chair and asked them to pray for me to receive. The officers laid hands on me and prayed to the Father in Jesus' name and asked Him to baptize me in the Holy Spirit.

About two weeks later beside my bed at prayer time, the evidence came forth, and I was speaking in a new language that I did not know or understand. I found out from the Bible that this was my spirit person, praying to God. I found out that I could interpret some of the things that my spirit was saying. Sometimes it would be praising the Lord or praying for things that my mind did not know that I needed. Praying was so much easier. I wanted to pray for every person that I saw. I loved people so much more and I loved the Lord so much more. It was an awesome change in my life.

Joel's prophecy which Peter speaks about in Acts 2:15-21 is found in Joel chapter 3, the first five verses. Peter 2:15-16 says "These people are not drunk, as you suppose, for it is only nine o'clock in the morning. No, this is what was spoken by the prophet Joel." Joel's prophecy was written about the year 400 B.C.

In Acts 1:4-5 Jesus is telling them and this is a command---"not to leave Jerusalem: 'Wait, rather, for the fulfillment of my Father's promise, of which you have heard me speak. John baptized with water, but within a few days you will be baptized with the Holy Spirit.'"

In Acts 1:8 the word says, "You will receive power when the Holy Spirit comes down on you; then you are to be my witnesses in Jerusalem, throughout Judea and Samaria, yes, even to the ends of the earth."

Acts 2:4 says, "And they were all filled with the Holy Spirit and began to speak in different tongues, as the Spirit enabled them to proclaim." This was when the 120 were in the upper room, on the day of Pentecost.

In Acts 1:4-5 Jesus told them not to go out to preach and minister until they had this Holy Spirit power, which is a supernatural power, to be agents and ambassadors of the Lord Jesus Christ.

In John 14:12 Jesus is saying, "Amen, amen, I say to you, whoever believes in me will do the works that I do, and will do greater ones than these, because I am going to the father." In the word it tells us that even Jesus needed this Holy Spirit power, and how He received it.

In Acts 10:38 it says, "How God anointed Jesus of Nazareth with the Holy Spirit and power. He went about doing good and healing all those oppressed by the devil, for God was with him."

If a person had this power, the ministry gifts would operate in his life. If he did not have this power the ministry gifts would not work in his life and ministry. These ministry gifts which go along with the Baptism of the Holy Spirit are listed in I Corinthians 12:8-9:

"To one is given through the Spirit the expression of wisdom; to another the expression of knowledge according to the same Spirit; to another, faith by the same Spirit; to another gifts of healing by the one Spirit; to another mighty deeds; to another prophecy; to another discernment of spirits; to another varieties of tongues; to another interpretation of tongues. But one and the same Spirit produces all of these, distributing them individually to each person as he wishes."

We must learn about spiritual things the same as we learn about physical things. Praying in tongues is called praying in the Spirit because it is our spirit that is praying to God. How do we know when we have the Holy Spirit baptism? The answer that I have always heard from people with much experience like Brother David DuPlessis is this:

Tongues are the least of the gifts of the Holy Spirit, and it is the first one that you receive. At the time of speaking in an unknown language, tongues, you will know that you have the Baptism of the Holy Spirit.

Also, you must have salvation before you can receive the baptism in the Holy Spirit.

Two thousand years ago we needed this awesome Holy Spirit power to get the church started.

In the fifth and sixth centuries and later, St. Patrick,

Columba, Brendan, and many others needed this Holy Spirit power for the mighty evangelistic works that they did. That is why they had the success that they had during that period of time in Ireland and Scotland.

Sometime after that the Holy Spirit Baptism died out in the Church of Rome. In August of 1960 it came back into the hierarchy of the Church.

In March of 1967, it came back into the Church for our laymen, with a group of students at Notre Dame University and for another group about the same time at Duquesne. Father Ralph Diorio lives in Worcester, Massachusetts, and has a healing ministry there. Since he has the Baptism of the Holy Spirit with the evidence of speaking in tongues, the gifts of the Holy Spirit operate in his life. One of the gifts that he has is the gift of healing, because thousands of people have been healed by miracles in his ministry. The gift of the word of knowledge or expression of knowledge also operates in his life.

In 1985, Full Gospel Business Men's Fellowship International had a South Carolina State Convention in Greenville. Father Ralph Diorio was one of our speakers. By this supernatural gift, he knew that there were ten ladies at the convention who had been raped, and they were never able to tell anyone that it had happened to them. It was a great burden in their lives. He called them to come up and he prayed for them and it relieved this terrible burden that they had. When he called them forward, only nine came for a long while. I believe the tenth one finally came for prayer.

When Jesus met the woman at the well and was talking to her, and told her that she had five husbands. The

Holy Spirit gift of the word of knowledge operated in His life and that is how He knew. I believe that all of the gifts of the spirit operated in Jesus' life. How can you know the answer? In Acts 10:38 the word tells us God anointed Jesus with the Holy Spirit and power. Everyone who has this Holy Spirit baptism has these gifts available in his or her life.

In my parish church the pastor would not have anything to do with the charismatic group. We were told if we wanted to be involved, that we would have to go to a small parish church that was about ten miles away from our church. This was about 1973-74.

The Holy Spirit led me to a group called "Full Gospel Business Men's Fellowship International." This was an interdenominational group of Christians that was very active at that time and still is today. Our big thing was evangelistic work. Today, we are in 160 countries. The leadership in this fellowship is required to have the Baptism in the Holy Spirit. Many Catholics come to our meetings. Many have received salvation and Holy Spirit baptism there.

Since December of 1973, I have had all these years of experience in evangelism. Now the Holy Spirit is showing me how and what to do, and leading me to do this kind of work in my church.

I know that there was confusion, disruption and all kinds of problems in the church during the time of the charismatic renewal. There was a reason for these problems and difficulties. First, the devil did not like it because so many were receiving salvation during that period of time.

Many were trying to receive the baptism in the Holy Spirit, and they could not receive it right away. They found out that they had to have salvation before they could receive the Holy Spirit baptism.

The big part of the problem was that so many of the lay people, not the bishops and priests, were receiving this blessing. They were receiving it among themselves and at prayer meetings in other denominations. The normal leadership, in the parishes and churches, much of the time, were not leading the charismatic meetings. This made for an awkward situation. The normal leadership really could not be the leadership because they were not in actuality a part of the renewal. This is what happened, time and time again, during this period of time called the "charismatic renewal."

Today, the situation is different and if it is followed through the results would be different. It would be different because the bishops and priests or pastors would be in their normal leadership role. The confusion would not be there as in the early charismatic renewal.

The Holy Spirit and the leadership at the Vatican are calling for an evangelistic outreach in the Church of Rome. I have pointed to a number of scriptures that are strong medicine. They really are gos-pills.

If the church, the Great Sleeping Giant, would look again at the Word of God, hear and increase her faith, believing, now seeing, not through a dark veil, but brightly, through this spiritual discernment, called the Baptism in the Holy Spirit, what a difference it would be. This is where the power is to move problems. This is where the answers are; the Lord has them and church leaders would hear them.

Luke 11:28 says, "...blessed are those who hear the Word of God and keep it," and if we are doers of the Word, the job will get done.

"If God be for us, who can be against us?" (Romans 8:31)

We have a big job to do in order to take care of the problem shown by the Holy Spirit.

Evangelization is a big job. It will not get done by itself. With the power of the Holy Spirit, He will certainly show us how and He will make the burden light.

Some concluding scripture verses came to me from Zechariah 4:6-9:

Then he said to me, "This is the Lord's message to Zerubbabel: not by an army, nor by might, but by my Spirit, says the Lord of Hosts. What are you, O great mountain? Before Zerubbabel you are but a plain. He shall bring out the capstone amid exclamations of 'Hail, Hail' to it."
"This word of the Lord then came to me: the hands of Zerubbabel have laid the foundations of this house, and his hands shall finish it; then you shall know that the Lord of hosts has sent me to you."

It is also my only desire: you shall know the Lord of hosts!

"Yet an hour is coming, and is already here, when authentic worshipers will worship the Father in Spirit and truth. Indeed, it is just worshipers the father seeks." (John 4:23)

A MAN CALLED GEORGE

Appendix

The Robe of Righteousness

HOW TO RECEIVE SALVATION

In Ephesians 2:8-9 it says, "For by <u>grace</u> are you saved through <u>faith</u>; and that is not from you; it is the gift of God; it is not from works, so no one may boast."

This scripture is not telling us whether you are saved, or whether you are not, it is telling us how you got saved if you are already saved, and if you are not saved, it is telling the way that you will get there! You need to read other scriptures about salvation to put it in perspective.

The key which unlocks all of the promises of God is as follows. Jesus taught that a man must be born again. The following four scriptures are statements from Jesus.

1.   "No one can see the Kingdom of God without being born from above." (John 3:3)

2.   "No one can enter the Kingdom of God without being born of water and Spirit." (John 3:5)

What is the water of the new birth? Does it refer to being baptized in water? Does that save you? No, that is not what Jesus is talking about. The Word of God is the water referred to in John 3:5. Let's prove that by looking through a number of Scriptures.

Ephesians 5:26, "to sanctify her (the church), cleansing her by the bath of water with the Word."

John 6:63, "It is the Spirit that gives life, while the flesh is of no avail. The words I have spoken to you are spirit and life."

John 15:3, "You are already pruned (another translation says "clean through the Word") because of the Word that I spoke to you."

John 17:17, "Consecrate them in the truth. Your word is truth."

I Peter 1:23, "You have been born anew, not from perishable, but from imperishable seed, through the living and abiding Word of God."

James 1:18, "He willed to give us birth by the Word of truth that we may be a kind of first fruits of his creatures."

A person must believe what the Word of God says about man. It says man is a sinner and that Christ died to save him from all sin. So if man will confess his sins to God and turn from sin with a whole heart and believe the Gospel, he is conforming to the Word of God. The Holy Spirit will then transform his life by the power of the Word of God and by the blood of Christ. That moment he is born from above.

This new creation, the newly born child of God is then to believe the Word of God and walk accordingly. He must begin to read the Bible and pray to God. He needs to walk and live in the Spirit and be conformed to the Word of God as he receives light.

3.   "Unless you turn and become like children, you will not enter the kingdom of heaven." (Matthew 18:3)

4.   "But I tell you, if you do not repent, you will all perish…" (Luke 13:3,5)
"The Lord does not delay his promise, as some regard 'delay,' but he is patient with you, not wishing that any should perish but that all should come to repentance." (II Peter 3:9)

In the above scriptures and others, the Lord says that salvation is a gift. He shows us that this gift is conditional. He does not want any to perish, but wants all to come into salvation. The following six steps of salvation scriptures show us what man must do to accept and receive this gift of salvation. These are the conditions the Lord says in His Word that we should meet. Now some have met these conditions through their everyday prayer life, but many have not.

Don't take the attitude that you cannot be deceived. Don't take the attitude that your church is the only right one and that it cannot mislead you. Your church may be right in its teachings concerning the New Birth. But make certain by going to the Bible yourself, and seeing with your own eyes, and knowing with your own heart, that you are right with God, that you have the real new birth, and that you are living a right walk with God.

There is no purpose served in fooling yourself. You are either born again, or you are not. You are either really saved, or you are being deceived into thinking you are, and you are lost.

You know your own true situation with God. If you

are not sure of your salvation, read the following scriptures and pray the salvation prayer MEANINGFULLY. The Lord Jesus has said in His Word that He will come into your heart, take over your life, be the Lord of your life, and you will have salvation.

The following two scriptures tell us how to receive a spiritual gift. In Matthew 7:7 and Luke 11:9 the Word tells you how to receive a spiritual gift.

"Ask, and you will receive. Seek, and you will find. Knock, and it will be opened to you." (Matthew 7:7)

"And I tell you, ask and you will receive; seek and you will find; knock and the door will be opened to you." (Luke 11:9)

When you read the six scriptural steps to salvation, read them out loud so you can hear them, and it will be a greater help to you. Why should you do this? In Ephesians 2:8-9 the Word tells us that you need faith to receive salvation. If your faith is low or weak, there is only one way to increase your faith.

In Romans 10:17 it tells us, "Thus faith comes from what is heard, and what is heard comes through the Word of Christ."

The more you hear the word of God, the stronger your faith becomes.

In Mark 16:16, it tells us that we must believe to be saved. That includes believing both ways, with your mind and with your spirit. If you only believe with your mind, all that you have is mental assent, and not salvation. When you pray the prayer of salvation, or some call it the sinner's prayer, pray it out loud, so that you can hear it with your ear. This helps you to believe it in your spirit man, and then you are a believer and you have won that part of the battle for salvation.

SIX SCRIPTURAL STEPS TO SALVATION

Remember, I am using the New American Bible version of the Holy Bible.

STEP 1:
"All men have sinned and are deprived of the glory of God." Romans 3:23

"...O God, be merciful to me, a sinner." Luke 18:13

STEP 2:
"...you will all come to the same end unless you reform." Luke 13:3

"Reform your lives! Turn to God, that your sins may be wiped away!" Acts 3:19

STEP 3:
"But if we acknowledge our sins, he who is just can be trusted to forgive our sins and cleanse us from every wrong." I John 1:9

"For if you confess with your lips that Jesus is Lord, and believe in your heart that God raised him from the dead, you will be saved." Romans 10:9

STEP 4:
"Let the scoundrel forsake his way, and the wicked man his thoughts; let him turn to the Lord for mercy; to our God, who is generous in forgiving." Isaiah 55:7

STEP 5:
"Yes, God so loved the world that he gave his only Son, that whoever believes in him may not die, but may have eternal life." John 3:16

"The man who believes in it and accepts baptism will be saved; the man who refuses to believe in it will be condemned." Mark 16:16

STEP 6:
"To his own he came, yet his own did not accept him. Any who did accept him he empowered to become children of God. These are they who believe in his name." John 1:11-12

SALVATION PRAYER

There is no "magical" prayer that helps you to receive salvation. God looks upon your heart. So do your best to just verbalize what you want to feel in your heart. I recommend a prayer like this:

Lord Jesus, I believe you died for my sins, and I ask you for your forgiveness from all unrighteousness. I renounce Satan, and all his works. I repent of my old ways, and I turn towards you, Jesus. I ask you now to come into my heart and take over my life. I surrender to you and I receive you now, as Lord and Savior of my life. Father, in Jesus' name, I pray, and I thank you, amen.

There is only one perfect person in the history of the world; that is Jesus Christ. He was sinless. Guess what? You are a human being. No matter how "spiritual" you would like to be, you were still born a sinner. Yes, you are a sinner by nature. Only by grace through faith do you receive eternal life with Jesus Christ.

God sees the sincerity of your heart. Although we should live a holy lifestyle, we are not perfect. God looks upon your heart, which is your spirit person, not a list of "do's" or "don'ts" in your everyday life.

Permit me to recommend some basic ways that you can GROW in your new walk with Jesus Christ.

"Grow rather in grace, and in the knowledge of our Lord and Savior Jesus Christ."   - II Peter 3:18

1.   Read a portion of the Bible each day! If you do not own a Bible, obtain one immediately. God's Word is your "road map" for your new life. The truths found in these scriptures will greatly assist you in your spiritual growth. Remember, no one has "arrived." Everyone learns SOMETHING NEW whenever he reads the Bible. God can show you new and wonderful things, simply by reading the Bible every day.

"Within my heart I treasure your promise, that I may not sin against you." (Psalm 119:11)

2.   Spend some time praying and worshipping the Lord each day! Through prayer, God can speak to you and strengthen you. He can personally visit you if you will spend meaningful time in His presence. Prayer is simply talking to God. Don't forget to spend time listening for God to speak to you!

"Never cease praying, render constant thanks; such is God's will for you in Christ Jesus." (I Thessalonians 5:17-18)

3.   Attend church regularly and continue with balance. As you participate regularly, you will be encouraged in your daily walk with the Lord Jesus Christ. Others will assist you to grow in the knowledge of His ways.

"We should not absent ourselves from the assembly, as some do, but encourage one another; and this all the more because you see that the Day draws near."
Hebrews 10:25

4.   Tell others about your new relationship with Jesus Christ. This is the most important thing ever to happen in your life. This is a step you have taken that has eternal implications!

"...Go home to your family and make it clear to them how much the Lord in his mercy has done for you."
Mark 5:19

5.   Fellowship with Christian people and friends who will help you (not hurt you) grow as a Christian. Spend time with people who think Godly thoughts. Spend time with people, maybe even new people, who will help to build you up, spiritually. Do not waste your time spending an excessive amount of time with people who gossip and back-bite and who will be a detriment to you, spiritually.

"The just man shall flourish like the palm tree, like a cedar of Lebanon shall he grow."
Psalm 92:13

JESUS CHRIST
THE BAPTIZER
IN THE HOLY SPIRIT

In 1976 at the Montreat Bible Conference I became acquainted with Brother David DuPlessis. He spoke to the entire crowd the first night. Then he had three two-hour sessions during the Conference which I attended. Here are some words of Brother David in this text.

JESUS CHRIST, THE BAPTIZER

"There was a man sent form God, whose name was John...The next day John seeth Jesus coming unto him, and saith, Behold the Lamb of God, which taketh away the sin of the world...And John bare record, saying, I saw the Spirit descending from heaven like a dove, and it abode upon him.

"And I knew him not: but he that sent me to baptize with water, the same said unto me, Upon whom thou shalt see the Spirit descending, and remaining upon him, the same is he which baptizeth with the Holy Ghost.

"And I saw, and bare record that this is the Son of God." (John 1:6,29,32-34).

Every one of the four Gospels spells out John's declaration, "I indeed baptize you with water; he shall baptize you with the Holy Ghost." When the Pharisees asked, "Why baptizeth thou?" he replied, "That he should be made manifest...therefore I am come baptizing with water." (John 1:25, 31). Furthermore, John assured them that he was sent to baptize with water (verse 33). It was his ministry. This fact was recognized to such an extent that he became known as "John the Baptist."

I doubt whether one could find a ten-year-old in Christendom that has not yet learned about John the Baptist. All through the ages, generation after generation, men have learned of this great prophet, but they know him by what he did and not by what he said or prophesied. Yet we know that he was both prophet and baptizer.

In recent times I have been astonished to find that very few Christians have ever heard that Christ is the baptizer in the Holy Ghost. They know Him as the Lamb of God, as Saviour; and as the Son of God, our Lord; but they are unfamiliar with the fact that He was announced to the world as the One to whom God gave the ministry of baptizing with the Holy Ghost.

Jesus Christ is both Saviour and Baptizer. We have no doubt that he is as much the Saviour today as when He died on Calvary as the Lamb of God. Even so, He is still the Baptizer in the Holy Spirit as much as He was when He commended this ministry on the day of Pentecost, for He is the "same, yesterday, today and forever."

The first intimation in history that a baptism with the Spirit was a possible event in the life of a human being came from John the Baptist. However, he did not announce the experience but rather the one who gave such an experience. He announced that the Baptizer was coming. He clearly states that God had told him that Christ would be the Baptizer with the Holy Ghost. He also assures us that the image for this act of Christ was his own act of baptizing in the river. From the very beginning, therefore, all John's converts fully expected an experience that would be as overwhelming as their baptism in the river. These converts had an encounter with the baptizer and not with water or even the river. What they were to expect was an encounter with the Baptizer in the Holy Spirit and not with the Spirit or with the work of the Spirit in their lives.

For every baptism there must be an agent to baptize, and an element with or into which to baptize, and finally a candidate to be baptized. Such a candidate must present himself and ask for baptism. Then there must be a total and complete surrender to the baptizer and not to the element in which he baptizes. The baptism in the Holy Spirit is an encounter with Christ, the Baptizer. The candidates are those who have already had an encounter with Him as the Lamb of God, the Saviour, who took away all their sin and made them worthy temples of the Holy Spirit.

The disciples who left John and followed Christ that He might baptize them with the Holy Spirit discovered that He was full of the Spirit. They saw His miracles to prove it and heard His word to confirm it. Then He gave them power and authority to cast out devils and heal the sick, but that was not the baptism in the Spirit that they expected. Finally they saw Him weak and as a Lamb led to the slaughter, and He opened not His mouth. He died on the cross and was laid in the tomb, and no one had been baptized in the Spirit. What about John's prophecy? Was it all mythical or mystical?

In the evening of that first Easter day of Resurrection, He suddenly and unexpectedly appeared in their midst. Then He breathed on them and said, "Receive ye the Holy Ghost." This was after He had explained, "As my Father hath sent me, even so send I you." But how did His Father send Him? First He came, born of the Spirit

(Luke 1:35), and then He was endued with the Spirit (Luke 4:1) to commence His earthly ministry. So here the disciples became the very first members of a new body, the church. He breathed eternal life into them. Calvary, the all-effective altar of God, had dealt with the sin question, and those who were dead in trespasses and sin now could receive the life-giving, regenerating Holy Spirit. This was for them the occasion where they were baptized into one body by the Spirit (I Corinthians 12:13).

But John said that God has said that Jesus would baptize with the Spirit, not that He would give the Spirit. I wonder how these disciples thought and felt about all these strange things? However, a few weeks later Jesus again spoke to the same men to whom He had said, "Receive ye the Holy Ghost." Now He confirms John's message. He says to them, "John truly baptized with water: but ye shall be baptized with the Holy Ghost not many days hence" (Acts 1:5). Here Christ accepts and confirms the same image that God had given to John, a baptism in water and a baptism in the Holy Spirit—indeed a river baptism, but the river of life must first begin to flow upon earth.

Several predictions were confirmed on the Day of Pentecost. The Father gave the promised Holy Ghost, who was heard as wind and seen as fire. Jesus began to baptize in the Spirit and fire. The immediate consequence of this baptism was that the candidates began to speak with other tongues, as Jesus had promised (Mark 16:17). Then the Holy Spirit began to convict of sin, righteousness and judgment as Peter preached to the multitude (John 16:8). But the record says, "They were all filled (overflowed) with the Holy Ghost, and (proof of which was) they began to speak with other tongues as the Spirit gave them utterance" (Acts 2:4).

It seems that from this very day onward much more emphasis was given to the experience of the disciples than to the act of Jesus the Baptizer, and the whole controversy began to revolve around glossolalia—speaking with other tongues—which was the very simple consequence of this baptism in the Spirit. The Holy Spirit was the gift and tongues was the consequence. These tongues were a manifestation of the Holy Spirit and not a manifestation of the ecstasy of the human spirit. Speaking in tongues by the Holy Spirit or, as Paul puts it, "Praying with the Spirit," is an act of the Holy Spirit upon the human spirit which transcends the understanding (I Corinthians 14:14-15).

Thus it seems clear that on the day of Pentecost the spirit of the disciples was baptized into the Holy Spirit and their bodies were filled with the Holy Spirit—overflowed with the Holy Spirit. The fact that they commenced to speak "with the Spirit" was proof of this overflowing.

In our day many pray for an infilling, an experience, instead of seeking the Baptizer. They ask the Holy Spirit to fill them when they should be asking Christ to baptize them. The baptism will produce the filling. This filling of the body by the baptism of the human spirit into the Holy Spirit produces an overflowing (see John 7:38) which causes the vocal organs to go into action and speak a language that is unknown to the candidate. He may be fully aware of what he is doing but does not know what he is saying (I Corinthians 14:14).

On the day of Pentecost God gave the Holy Spirit and Christ then baptized His followers into the Spirit, and they began to speak with other tongues as the Spirit gave them utterance (Acts 2:4). About ten years later, according to Acts 10:44-46, when the Apostle Peter dared to preach to the Gentiles for the first time (Acts 11:19), these same Gentiles received exactly the same experience that the apostles and the disciples of Christ had on the day of Pentecost. The record says, "And they of the circumcision (the Jews) were astonished, as many as came with Peter, because that on the Gentiles also was poured out the gift of the Holy Ghost.

For they heard them speak with tongues, and magnify God" (Acts 10:46). The Jewish Christians in Jerusalem objected to all this (Acts 11:2). Then Peter in his defense said, "And as I began to speak, the Holy Ghost fell on them, as on us at the beginning. Then remembered I the word of the Lord, how that he said, John indeed baptized with water, but ye shall be baptized with the Holy Ghost" (Acts 11:15,16). In other words, it was the same Baptizer who baptized into the same element, with the same consequences. The consequences were what convinced the Jewish Christians that the experience of the Gentiles was valid, for they heard them speak with tongues (Acts 10:46).

From this record it is quite clear that during the first decade Peter and the church in Jerusalem believed that Jesus is the Baptizer in the Holy Spirit and that "speaking with tongues" was the immediate consequence or confirmation of this baptism. During this last decade in our time the Christian world has become more conscious of the Holy Spirit and many are reaching out for His power and a charismatic ministry. However, it seems to me that unless the church once again lifts up Christ as the Baptizer, many will seek the blessing from the Holy Spirit and fail to find it because He will always honor Christ.

To get the baptism in the Spirit everyone must seek an encounter with the Baptizer, who began this ministry on the day of Pentecost when He truly came back in the Spirit to baptize His disciples. He is the same, yesterday, today and forever (Hebrews 13:8).

HOW TO RECEIVE
THE BAPTISM
IN THE HOLY SPIRIT

Jesus promised the abundant and fruitful life as a result of being baptized in the Holy Spirit.

The results of this baptism are that God will give you power and love!

POWER – to live the Christian life.
Acts 1:8 "You will receive power when the Holy Spirit comes down on you; then you are to be my witnesses in Jerusalem, throughout Judea and Samaria, yes, even to the ends of the earth."

LOVE – to love others beyond your own ability.
John 15:12 "This is my commandment: love one another as I have loved you."

WE RECEIVE THE BAPTISM BY ASKING

Luke 11:13 "If you, with all your sins, know how to give your children good things, how much more will the heavenly Father give the Holy Spirit to those who ask him."

JESUS CHRIST IS THE BAPTIZER

Mark 1:7,8 "The theme of his preaching was: 'One more powerful than I is to come after me. I am not fit to stoop and untie his sandal straps. I have baptized you in water; he will baptize you in the Holy Spirit.'"

WE MUST PRAY WITH
A SINCERE ATTITUDE

Acts 2:38-39 "...You must reform and be baptized, each one of you, in the name of Jesus Christ, that your sins may be forgiven; then you will receive the gift of the Holy Spirit. It was to you and your children that the promise was made, and to all those still far off whom the Lord our God calls."

RENOUNCE: bitterness, unforgiveness, hatred, evil thoughts, resentments.

RENOUNCE: all occult involvement.

RENOUNCE: Satan's works, and command him to depart, in Jesus' name.

ASK GOD: for the Holy Spirit, for Jesus Christ to baptize you.

LET'S PRAY:

Dear Father God, I come before You in Jesus' name...I believe in my heart, and confess with my mouth, that He is Lord...I now renounce all sin in my life, any bitterness, unforgiveness, hatred, or evil thoughts that I am holding toward anyone. (Name to God any names that He reveals to you.)...I renounce all involvement in the occult. In Jesus' name, I command Satan to depart...Father, forgive me of these sins and cleanse my heart, through the blood of Jesus which was shed on the cross for me...Father, I ask You to give me the Holy Spirit, and, Lord Jesus, baptize me in the Holy Spirit...I receive the baptism in the Holy Spirit now by faith. In Jesus' name I pray...Amen.

YOU CAN RECEIVE THE HOLY SPIRIT

Acts 2:38 "...you will receive the gift of the Holy Spirit."

YOU CAN PRAY IN TONGUES

Acts 2:4 "All were filled with the Holy Spirit. They began to express themselves in foreign tongues and make bold proclamation as the Spirit prompted them."

...AND IN GOD'S WILL

Romans 8:26-27 "The Spirit too helps us in our weakness, for we do not know how to pray as we ought; but the Spirit himself makes intercession for us with groanings that cannot be expressed in speech. He who searches hearts knows what the Spirit means, for the Spirit intercedes for the saints as God himself wills."

YOU CAN BUILD UP YOUR FAITH

Jude 20 "But you, beloved, grow strong in your holy faith through prayer in the Holy Spirit."

YOU CAN PRAY IN TONGUES AT ALL TIMES

Ephesians 6:18 "At every opportunity pray in the Spirit, using prayers and petitions of every sort. Pray constantly and alternatively for all in the holy company."

NOW...BEGIN TO PRAISE THE LORD!

Lift up your head, lift up your hands...
Tell Jesus you love Him.

Then thank your heavenly father for filling you with His power and His love.

Thank Him right now for your new prayer language.

Praise Him and thank Him in English.

Now praise Him more…

Begin to speak in tongues to God, in Jesus' name…praise Him again. Tell Him out loud you love Him. Again, speak in the Spirit unto God. Praise the Lord!

LET GOD'S WORD ASSURE YOU THAT YOU HAVE NOW RECEIVED THE BAPTISM IN THE HOLY SPIRIT

Reread Acts 2:38-39 and Luke 11:13.

DO NOT DOUBT praying in tongues. It is real. If you're not praying freely, you will. Just keep praising the Lord!

YOU DO NOT HAVE TO TARRY, agonize, or beg God. Remember Luke 11:13. He gave you the Holy Spirit by your asking Him.

MAKE A FULL COMMITMENT. The last thing we give up to God is our mouth and tongue. So get your mind on Jesus, and give Him your entire being (including your tongue).

THERE'S SO MUCH MORE GOD HAS FOR YOU!

POWER TO WITNESS

Acts 4:31 "The place where they were gathered shook as they prayed. They were filled with the Holy Spirit and continued to speak God's word with confidence."

...AND MANY OTHER GIFTS!
I Corinthians 12:1-11
"...wisdom...knowledge...faith...healing...
working of miracles...prophecy...distinguishing between
spirits...different kinds of tongues...interpretation of
tongues..."

GOD HAS GIVEN YOU THE FRUIT OF HIS SPIRIT.
USE THESE TO GLORIFY JESUS IN YOUR LIFE

Galatians 5:22,23 "...the fruit of the spirit is love,
joy, peace, patient endurance, kindness, generosity, faith,
mildness, and chastity. Against such there is no law!"

GOD'S PROMISES GO ON AND ON!

I Corinthians 2:9 "...Eye has not seen, ear has not
heard, nor has it so much as dawned on man what God has
prepared for those who love him."

Links of encouragement:

www.fgbmfi.org

sardugg@aol.com

INDEX

NOTES

NOTES

If this book has inspired or challenged you, please let me know. If you have any questions or need spiritual help or guidance, please feel free to write to me your comments or your questions.

Mr. George M. Duggan, Jr.
46 Queen Street #12
Charleston, SC 29401